aul Hinton

DayOne

Paul Hinton has given his life to reaching out and proclaiming the gospel to non-Christians. If you want help in personal evangelism which is straightforward, biblical, practical and focused on Jesus, this is the book for you. All Christians should read and put into practice the things taught here!

Roger Carswell, evangelist, UK

Paul Hinton ponders a lifetime of both personal and 'up-front' evangelism and distils those insights into this warm-hearted, biblical, urgent, realistic and practical book. I found myself challenged and inspired to reach out much more intentionally than I do. It will hold the attention of the most reluctant evangelist and would be the ideal preparation for Christian Unions or churches embarking on mission. I commend it with great enthusiasm.

Richard Cunningham, Director, Universities and Colleges Christian Fellowship (UCCF)

First printed 2016
ISBN 978-1-84625-560-1

A CIP record is held at the British Library

Published by Day One Publications, Ryelands Road, Leominster, HR6 8NZ
☎ 01568 613 740
FAX 01568 611 473

email—sales@dayone.co.uk
web site—www.dayone.co.uk

Cover design by Rob Jones, Elk Design
Printed by TJ International

For Fiona, my wonderful wife,
who has put up with my absences
due to my many years on the
road as an evangelist.
I couldn't have done any of it
without her support, love and sacrifice.

ACKNOWLEDGEMENTS

I am very grateful to Mike Smith, who checked the manuscript and made many helpful comments. Thanks also to Roger Carswell, who offered advice from the wealth of his writing experience and at a broader level has been a great mentor in evangelism over many years.

Contents

Introduction: A master class

Life-saving is by definition a very serious business. It's a big responsibility. Those who are entrusted with the job need to have the right training and motivation. My family and I have spent many holidays by the seaside. I am always reassured by the sight of the young men and women in bright red and yellow uniforms on lifeguard duty. They are not there (we hope) to get a tan, play games or catch up on the latest gossip. They are there to save the lives of men, women and children who at any time might need their help. Becoming a lifeguard is not easy; it takes long hours of training, with courses to attend and manuals to read and learn. I am glad it is taken that seriously because one day my life or the life of my wife or children may depend on it.

Every Christian is in the life-saving business. We have been entrusted with the vitally important responsibility of leading people from death to life. To be honest, though, it is not something I have always taken seriously. Sometimes life feels like a beach full of smiling, happy people having a good time and in no danger at all. But the truth is that people are spiritually lost and in real danger of eternal death. We Christians have the only message that will save them, and God has given us the job of reaching out to a lost world with this saving gospel. Just like lifeguards, we need the right training and motivation, and that is what this book is all about. We have a lifesavers' manual, the Bible, and in this book we are going to look at one chapter in John's Gospel that is packed full of instructions on how to save a life.

THE PASSAGE: JOHN 4:4–42

It began as an ordinary, everyday chat about a cold drink on a hot day, and ended as an extraordinary conversation about eternal life. We don't know exactly how long they talked together that day—possibly only a matter of minutes—but the repercussions of that conversation were massive. The ripples spread out to a town, and beyond that to the whole world. Such was the meeting between Jesus and an unnamed Samaritan woman.

Jesus is on his way from Judea, in the south of Israel, to Galilee, in the north. In between was the region of Samaria. It is midday. It is hot. Jesus and his disciples are tired and hungry after a long morning's walk. They have stopped at a well just outside the town of Sychar, in the heart of Samaria. The disciples have gone into the town to buy food, leaving Jesus alone at the well. As he rests there waiting for the disciples to return, a woman from the nearby town approaches, carrying a water pot.

The conversation begins with a simple request: Jesus asks the woman to give him a drink. Now that in itself is a shock. She can see that he is a Jew. Jews, as John points out in his commentary on the story (v. 9), would have nothing to do with Samaritans. In fact, they were two communities divided by generations of deep prejudice and hatred. The woman's curiosity is further aroused by this stranger's response: what's that about living water (v. 10)?

Now that Jesus has her attention, he begins to explain that he is offering her spiritual life. The water in the well is merely a picture of the vital, fulfilling, everlasting life he alone can give. She is thirsty for this life. She has known many disappointments, not least five failed marriages. She begins to realize that this is no ordinary Jew, especially as he seems to know all about her chequered past, even though they have never met before. Is he a prophet, or maybe something more? Jesus reveals his true identity: he is the Messiah, God's promised King. In that moment of realization, the woman's life is turned around. She is transformed from a disappointed and disillusioned woman into a joyful and fulfilled disciple.

At that point, the disciples return from their shopping expedition. They are amazed and confused to find Jesus talking to this unknown Samaritan woman. She leaves, maybe feeling uncomfortable under the disciples' scrutinizing gaze, and returns to the town, full of what that simple encounter with Jesus has meant.

Now Jesus turns to his bemused disciples and begins to teach them a lesson they will never forget, a lesson that will shape the rest of their lives. Jesus shows them that their number one priority must be this very work of reaching everyone they meet with the good news of new life. Getting stuck into the work of harvesting souls for eternal life is to be their life's work.

Over the next few chapters we are going to join the disciples on this crash course on witnessing. Jesus gives us both the secrets of motivation for this work and a wonderful and practical example of how to go about it. At the end of the passage, the woman herself becomes a beautifully simple model of witnessing. Very few of us find sharing our faith easy, but deep down most of us know it is important. This passage of Scripture is recorded to show us how to move from mere small talk to the big talk of the gospel, just as Jesus did.

1 Vision: Sharing God's vision for the world

Every year or so, I visit a particular building in a town near to where I live, and when I leave that place my view of the world is changed. It's my optician's. In John 4 Jesus gives his disciples an eye test. But it is not their physical eyesight he is interested in; it is their spiritual vision he is concerned about. Sadly, they fail the test. They just can't see why Jesus is talking with the Samaritan woman. After all, it's meal time, and added to that she is a Samaritan. To the disciples she is an irrelevant inconvenience getting in the way of their lunch. But to Jesus, she is a lost soul in desperate need of eternal life. The disciples look at this woman totally differently from Jesus. They can't see what he sees. They are spiritually short-sighted. Jesus says,

> Don't you have a saying, 'It's still four months until harvest'? I tell you, open your eyes and look at the fields! They are ripe for harvest' (John 4:35).

This is both a rebuke and a challenge. As Jesus speaks these words, he and the disciples are surrounded by agricultural land full of crops. All around them is a potential harvest. Bringing in that harvest on time is a massively important job: it is literally a matter of life and death. Jesus, as he so often does, uses the physical as an illustration of the spiritual. He wants them to see another crop that needs harvesting. This too is a serious matter, also literally a matter of life and death. The harvest surrounds them every day, if only they could see it. This is the spiritual harvest of the eternal souls of people. The woman they have so easily dismissed typifies the harvest they are in danger of missing.

'You are not looking at the world the way I do,' Jesus is saying. Jesus sees this woman as a lost person: thirsty for life, yet ignorant of where that life is to be found, looking in all the wrong places for fulfilment and satisfaction. She has had five failed marriages and now she is just living with a man. Maybe she has come to the conclusion that there is really no point in marrying if it's just going to end in divorce. She is living a sad, wasted life and heading to a lost eternity. Jesus's love for her is not blind. He sees her sin, knows all about her immoral living, yet he loves her just the same, and longs that she might find forgiveness and eternal life. That's how Jesus views people, and that's how he wants his followers to see people too.

On another occasion we read,

> When he saw the crowds, he had compassion on them, because they were harassed and helpless, like sheep without a shepherd (Matt. 9:36).

Jesus saw the crowds as vulnerable sheep without direction or protection—but is that how we view them?

THE VISION TEST

It's easy to be critical of the disciples, but how often do we fail the vision test?

Test one: It's 10 p.m. I'm just settling down in front of the TV news after a long day when the phone rings. At the other end of the line is a man who has just started coming to our church. He tells me he has a flat tyre and is stuck at the side of the road not far from my house. Somewhat reluctantly, I leave the house and find him. After some time, and several knocks and scrapes, we get the tyre changed. He is really grateful and he never forgets that simple act. He keeps coming to church and seems to really engage with the messages he hears.

Test two: I am travelling on the train to speak at a church weekend away. I have brought my laptop with me so I can use the journey time to do some much-needed admin. I'm hoping for a quiet table to myself, and I find one—great! Then an old lady shuffles into the carriage and sits down directly opposite me. I keep my head down, eyes fixed on the computer screen.

'Where are you going?' she asks.

I tell her.

'Really? I have a niece who lives there,' she replies. 'Is your trip business or pleasure?'

I look up. 'Business,' I say.

'What do you do?' she goes on.

'Why can't she leave me alone?' I think. 'I really wanted to get on with this work!' Reluctantly I stop tapping on the keyboard and explain. A conversation ensues which gives a great opportunity to share something of Christ.

Two tests I am sad to say I failed. That man and that woman were inconveniences to me. But how would Jesus have viewed them? He would have seen them just as he viewed the Samaritan woman: with a deep love and real concern.

THE PRIORITIES TEST

But it's not just an issue of vision; it's also one of priorities.

Because the disciples are not seeing people as Jesus—and therefore God—sees them, they do not share his priorities. At this point the disciples are thinking only of the food they had gone into the town to buy and are now ready to tuck into. Lunch is their number one priority, but it's not Jesus's priority.

> Meanwhile his disciples urged him, 'Rabbi, eat something.' But he said to them, 'I have food to eat that you know nothing about … My food,' said Jesus, 'is to do the will of him who sent me and to finish his work' (John 4:31–34).

Jesus is saying that this work of saving lost people is the most important and fundamental thing about him. It's the work he is totally committed to. It comes before everything else, even physical food. Again I ask myself: do I share that same priority in my life? It is so easy for other things, even trivial things, to take priority over reaching lost people. How often have I let my petty personal needs dictate, rather than the eternal needs of a dying world? It's not that we shouldn't take time out to rest and relax; it's rather that this shouldn't take first place. There are times when we should be willing to forgo those things because of the more important work of reaching others with the gospel.

THE OBEDIENCE TEST

In the previous chapter of John's Gospel, Jesus has a conversation with a man called Nicodemus, a religious leader. Jesus explains why his Father God sent him into the world. He says, 'For God did not send his Son into the world to condemn the world, but to save the world through him' (John 3:17). Jesus explains that God has sent him on a rescue mission. At the end of John's Gospel, the risen Jesus commissions his disciples:

> Again Jesus said, 'Peace be with you! As the Father has sent me, I am sending you.' And with that he breathed on them and said, 'Receive the Holy Spirit. If you forgive anyone's sins, their sins are forgiven; if you do not forgive them, they are not forgiven' (John 20:21–23).

Just as Jesus was sent by his Father, so now Jesus is sending his disciples. He was sent into the world on a mission; they are now being sent into the world with a mission—the same rescue mission. They are being sent out to proclaim the authentic and authoritative message of the forgiveness of sins for all who will repent and trust in Jesus. That mission is given to all Christians. And all true Christians have also received the Holy Spirit to empower them for thc task. There really is no excuse. Nothing should be more important to us than this work. In the end, it's not just a matter of vision and priorities, but ultimately of obedience. Every Christian is under orders to reach a lost world. We do have a responsibility for the lost souls around us. The apostle Paul often spoke of this sense of duty to preach Christ. He said:

> I am a debtor both to Greeks and non-Greeks, both to the wise and the foolish. That is why I am so eager to preach the gospel also to you who are in Rome (Rom. 1:14–15).

> For when I preach the gospel, I cannot boast, since I am compelled to preach. Woe to me if I do not preach the gospel! (1 Cor. 9:16).

We don't always feel a deep sense of desire to tell others

about Christ, but we should always have a deep sense of duty to do so.

It's not just we as individual witnesses who are being scrutinized here by Jesus; it's our corporate witness as churches, too. What vision do our churches have for reaching the lost? Does that vision inform and decide our priorities—how we spend our money, what activities we run, how we preach on a Sunday and what staff we employ? All these things should reflect our priority to reach the lost. Ultimately, we must ask ourselves: are our churches being obedient to the Lord of the harvest?

OUR RESPONSIBILITY AND THEIRS

It is important, however, to understand where our responsibility ends. You and I are responsible for taking the gospel to a lost world, but we are not responsible for people's response to the message. The apostle Paul understood exactly where his responsibility began and ended. In Acts 18 we read of what happened when Paul began to preach the gospel in Corinth:

> Paul devoted himself exclusively to preaching, testifying to the Jews that Jesus was the Messiah. But when they opposed Paul and became abusive, he shook out his clothes in protest and said to them, 'Your blood be on your own heads! I am innocent of it. From now on I will go to the Gentiles' (Acts 18:5–6).

Paul did feel a responsibility to preach the gospel to the Jews in Corinth, but once they had rejected his message, he knew he had discharged that responsibility and was free to move on to others. Paul was clear: the Jews were responsible to God for their rejection of the message.

If we are not clear what our responsibility is and isn't, it can lead to false guilt and feelings of failure. These feelings can cause us to give up witnessing altogether. Sad though it is, sometimes all we can do is share the message and move on, leaving the situation to God. Of course, we should continue to pray for those we have spoken to, and always be ready to speak to them again in the future, but we must not let a sense of guilt or failure paralyse us and prevent us from taking the gospel to others.

OUR RESPONSIBILITY AND GOD'S

It is also important to understand where our responsibility ends and God's begins. When Paul is describing his evangelistic ministry in 2 Corinthians 4, he is clear as to what his work is and what God's work is:

> By setting forth the truth plainly we commend ourselves to everyone's conscience in the sight of God. And even if our gospel is veiled, it is veiled to those who are perishing. The god of this age has blinded the minds of unbelievers, so that they cannot see the light of the gospel that displays the glory of Christ, who is the image of God. For what we preach is not ourselves, but Jesus Christ as Lord, and ourselves as your servants for Jesus' sake. For God who said, 'Let light shine out of darkness,' made his light shine in our hearts to give us the light of the knowledge of God's glory displayed in the face of Christ (2 Cor. 4:2–6).

Paul knew that his responsibility was honestly and plainly to preach Jesus, and it was God's responsibility to shine that truth into people's hearts. Paul understood that people have been blinded by Satan and that only a miraculous work of God, comparable to his work in creation, can enable them to see. You and I cannot make people believe, but we can and must share the message of the gospel. The rest is God's work—and what a relief that is!

A HARVEST FIELD, NOT A DESERT

There is also a word of real encouragement to us here. In John 4:35 Jesus tells his disciples to lift up their eyes and look at the fields, for they are ready for harvest. It is not a spiritual desert they are in, but a harvest field. They may have been tempted to see Samaria as a very unpromising place for a work of God, the very last place that would receive the Messiah. Yet that very thing was happening before the disciples' eyes. The woman had been converted and now, as Jesus spoke to his disciples, a crowd was making its way towards them from the village. The woman had rushed home with the exciting news of this unique man with divine knowledge, so the crowd had come to see for itself. The phrase 'ripe for harvest' in verse 35 could more literally be translated 'white for harvest', and some have suggested that this may have been a play on words with reference to this crowd of people dressed in long white robes and making their way towards them across the fields. Many in the town were to come to faith that day.

You might look at your friends or your town as equally unpromising, but remember: the world is a harvest field, not a desert. There will be results. If we will give ourselves to this work, God will give us a harvest of souls.

Personal or group study: Jonah 4

1. *Why did Jonah run from God's call to go and preach to the Ninevites? Compare Jonah 1:1–3 with Jonah 4:1–3.*

2. *How should the character of God inform our attitude to reaching others?*
3. *How did God use the leafy plant as an illustration of Jonah's selfish motives (Jon. 4:5–11).*
4. *What kinds of wrong priorities do we sometimes have that stop us giving our lives to the work of evangelism?*

(Suggested answers to these questions can be found in the Appendix.)

2 Barriers: Barrier-breakers and bridge-builders

I once saw two stickers in the rear window of a car. The first said, 'Have faith in God', while the other said, 'Keep your distance!' I am sure that whoever put them there didn't intend them to be read together like that, but I couldn't help feeling that they expressed what many Christians are saying to the world around them. We want to share our faith with non-Christians, but we don't want them to share our lives. The problem, however, is that evangelism cannot be done effectively from a distance.

On that hot, dusty day in first-century Samaria, Jesus sat down beside a well. On the surface, there was nothing unusual about that. Jesus was thirsty after a tiring morning's walk, and the well was the place you went for a drink. A woman from the nearby village joined Jesus at the well, and Jesus asked her for a drink and began to engage her in conversation. Again, nothing out of the ordinary in that either, you might think. Yet when we start to look a little deeper at what was happening there, it becomes clear that this was far from ordinary. In that one simple act Jesus smashed through massive ethnic, religious, social, moral and spiritual barriers; and if we are going to reach a lost world with the good news of eternal life, we too are going to need to be barrier-breakers.

THE RACE BARRIER

First, Christ broke through the race barrier. Samaritans were the product of mixed-race marriages. Many generations before the time of Christ, Jews had married non-Jews. The pure Jew regarded the Samaritan as a racial half-breed and as such as *persona non grata*. That's why the woman was so shocked that Jesus, a Jew, asked her for a drink and engaged her in conversation. Perhaps the nearest we might get to a comparable situation in recent history would be the segregation along racial lines in the deep south of America in the 1960s or the Unionist–Nationalist divide in Northern Ireland at the height of the Troubles. I don't think it was coincidence that took Jesus and his disciples into the heart of the region of Samaria and then caused Jesus to speak to this Samaritan woman. The disciples would have been brought up with all the Jewish prejudices against Samaritans. Jesus was teaching them that there is no place for prejudice with God. God loves the whole world, and Jesus came to be the Saviour of the whole world: for every race, tribe, tongue and nation. That is the very thing that the Samaritans of Sychar who came to believe in Jesus said:

> They said to the woman, 'We no longer believe just because of what you said; now we have heard for ourselves, and we know that this man really is the *Saviour of the world*' (John 4:42, emphasis added).

If Jesus loves the whole world without favourites, so should those who claim to follow him. Sadly, this has not always been the case. At times, Christians have been blatantly racist. Often, though, it is more subtle. Perhaps we just avoid or ignore people from other ethnic backgrounds. I remember leading a team in literature distribution in France. One lady on the team confided in another worker that she didn't really like the French—yet we were there to share the love of God for everyone!

THE RELIGION BARRIER

Then Jesus smashed through the religious barrier. The Samaritans had their own corrupted version of Judaism. They no longer went to the temple in Jerusalem to worship. They had set up their own place of worship on Mount Gerizim. This comes out in the question the Samaritan woman asks Jesus about where people should worship:

> Our ancestors worshipped on this mountain, but you Jews claim that the place where we must worship is in Jerusalem (v. 20).

Samaritans were really a Jewish cult, a bit like Mormonism is to Christianity. This had been a source of tension between Jews and Samaritans. Jesus patiently and lovingly led the woman out of her confusion and error. I have to admit there have been times when, having heard a knock at the door, I have looked out of the window and seen the Jehovah's Witnesses, and my heart has sunk, dreading the long conversation that would just be a 'waste of time'. To Jesus, no matter how awkward or difficult this woman may have been, she was not a waste of his time.

THE SOCIAL BARRIER

Then Jesus smashed the social barrier. It went completely against the social conventions of the day for a man to speak to a woman he didn't know. Jewish rabbis would not even teach women; women were regarded as totally inferior. As far as the rabbis were concerned, women were religious nobodies. Maybe that is also why the disciples were 'surprised' to find Jesus talking 'with a woman' (v. 27). Even today, many women struggle with feelings of inferiority, feelings often reinforced by the societies in which they live. How refreshing to see how different Jesus was from the rabbis of his day! To Jesus, this woman was a somebody, a precious individual made in God's image.

There may be many social barriers that get in the way of our sharing the good news. Perhaps it is the class or social status barrier. Often, the church has not been good at reaching people at each end of the social ladder—the poor or the very rich. Traditionally in the West, the evangelical church has been strong among the middle classes, and new churches are planted in these middle-class areas. In contrast, very little work has been done in the vast socially deprived areas of our cities.

I recently heard of tension among a number of churches over which church attracted the most students from the nearby university. It is hard to imagine the same scramble to attract the cleaners, bus drivers or the unemployed. Our vision for the lost can be very selective. If not consciously, then subconsciously we target people who come from 'nice', educated backgrounds. Some of this is a byproduct of the teaching of the church-growth gurus, who tell us that the most effective way to reach people is to target those who are similar to us. As most Christians are from the educated middle classes, this means we will never reach people from other backgrounds. The whole thing becomes a vicious circle, with more and more churches being started in relatively well-reached middle-class areas, while hardly anything is done to reach the poorer, less-educated communities. All of this seems far removed from the early church, where Paul could write to the church in Ephesus and address slaves and slave-owners in the same congregation.

CONSTANTLY ADAPTING

In 1 Corinthians Paul explains one of the principles upon which he based his missionary work:

> Though I am free and belong to no one, I have made myself a slave to everyone, to win as many as possible. To the Jews I became like a Jew, to win the Jews. To those under the law I became like one under the law (though I myself am not under the law), so as to win those under the law. To those not having the law I became like one not having the law (though I am not free from God's law but am under Christ's law), so as to win those not having the law. To the weak I became weak, to win the weak. I have become all things to all people so that by all possible means I might save some. I do all this for the sake of the gospel, that I may share in its blessings (1 Cor. 9:19–23).

Paul is saying that he is constantly changing in order to remove any possible barriers that might prevent him from reaching people for Christ. Of course there are certain things he will not change or compromise, such as the gospel message. Actually, it is for the sake of that unchanging gospel that he is willing to adapt to new cultural and social settings. Nothing must get in the way of winning as many as possible, says Paul.

This was a principle understood by Hudson Taylor when

he first went as a missionary to China. He took on the Chinese dress and haircut in order to make it easier for him to mix with, and be accepted by, the local population. Up until then, the missionary community had dressed in Western clothes. Many criticized Taylor, accusing him of compromise.

I sometimes wonder how this principle would change some of the ways we do church. When my wife and I were having our first child we were introduced to the home-from-home delivery suite. This was a hospital room arranged to look like an ordinary bedroom. Instead of cold clinical lights and furnishings, there were curtains at the windows, wallpaper on the walls, soft lighting and pine furniture. All the hospital equipment, such as gas bottles, was placed in cupboards out of sight. The whole idea behind this was that mothers-to-be would be more relaxed in this familiar environment and so the birth would be a better experience—although, as my wife pointed out, you are not admiring the furnishings when you are in labour! Whatever we might think of the effectiveness of this approach, we can admire the thinking behind it. But many people feel just as out of place and uncomfortable visiting church as they do hospital. It would be an interesting exercise to evaluate the ways we do things in our church, just as our local maternity ward did, and ask ourselves: what could we change to make the experience more accessible? Of course, just like the hospital, we are never going to get rid of the essentials that are at the heart of what we are there to do. A spiritual birth is just as important as a physical one and must be taken seriously, so we are not going to change anything that would compromise that. But there are many things we could and should change that would actually make us more effective in this important work.

What cultural and social barriers are getting in the way of our churches reaching the lost? Are we willing to sacrifice those cherished traditions and ways of doing things, in order to be more accessible to lost people?

THE MORAL AND SPIRITUAL BARRIER

The biggest barrier Jesus broke through was the moral and spiritual barrier. This woman's life was in a moral mess. She had probably been ostracized within her own community because of her lifestyle. That may well have been why she was drawing water in the heat of midday, rather than in the cool of the evening, when the rest of the townsfolk would have visited the well. Jesus knew all about the moral mess she was in, but that didn't put him off. She may have been living a life that was far from God's ideal, but God was not far from her. In fact, in the person of Jesus, God was far closer than she could ever have realized.

Sometimes as Christians, we are guilty of writing people off because of the sinful lifestyles they lead. I remember one training session on evangelism where an elder of a church admitted that he didn't really want to speak to his work colleagues about his faith because of the bad language they used. In another church, the pastor told me of the consternation among his members because a transvestite began attending the service. I know of one pastor who was asked to leave his church because he had welcomed prostitutes into his meetings.

When the Pharisees wanted to insult Christ, one of the

things they said about him was that he was 'the friend of sinners'. What an accusation! Little did they realize that it was one of the biggest compliments they could have given.

I have a friend who works for the Queen at Windsor Castle. His job is to look after and restore the furniture in her palaces. If you visit Windsor Castle as a tourist you can take a tour of some of the staterooms: they are spectacular, and full of amazing furniture. Great four-poster beds and ornate, finely carved chairs and tables, polished and gleaming, fill every room. To be honest, though, as impressive as it all is, it is hard to imagine living there. You would be scared to touch anything in case you spoilt it. You wouldn't dream of bouncing on the beds or putting your feet up on the sofas.

Of course, this is not where my friend works; he has a workshop, a room the tourists never see. It is very different from those fine staterooms. It's full of tools and furniture in various states of repair. I haven't visited his workshop, but I imagine tables with legs missing, chairs with the stuffing coming out, pots of polish, rags on the table and shavings on the floor. My friend and his colleagues spend weeks, even months, on a single piece of furniture, painstakingly repairing and restoring it. After the fire at Windsor Castle in 1992, they were busy for years, cleaning and repairing badly damaged furniture which had been blackened and scarred from the smoke and flames. Nothing was thrown away that could be rescued, restored and reclaimed. Some people's image of the church is like those polished and pristine staterooms: it's full of well-dressed and well-spoken people; perfect people who have it 'all together' in their lives (or at least, they think they do). They might imagine going to church being a bit like going to those staterooms: it's OK for a visit, but you wouldn't want to live there. You would feel uncomfortable, always scared of spoiling things. To be honest, sometimes we Christians have created this image.

I suggest that this is not how church should be. When we come to the New Testament, we see that church is much more like my friend's workshop: full of damaged people who have been scarred and burned by life, who have been rescued by Jesus and are now being repaired and restored. This work, too, is often slow and painstaking. And in the process, church is messy, and it has to be if it is to fulfil its God-given mission of rescue.

Just take a look at the Gospels, as they tell of the sorts of people to whom Jesus ministered. Many of them were the rejects and the reprobates of society, the weak and the marginalized of their communities. Think of the disciples he called: what a motley crew they were! Several were uneducated fishermen. One was a tax collector, and tax collectors were a notoriously corrupt bunch who had collaborated with the invading Roman army, and as a result were utterly despised by their community. Another had been a member of a violent political group called the Zealots. These disciples were not the most promising of material. Look how long it took Jesus to knock them into shape, as they struggled with all their misunderstandings and hang-ups.

Then read some of the letters of the New Testament and see the background of many of those first followers of Jesus. In 1 Corinthians 6 Paul gives a long list of the backgrounds from which some of these believers had been rescued: sexual immorality, idolatry, adultery and homosexuality. There were thieves, the greedy, drunkards, revellers and swindlers. In the same chapter, Paul has to address some serious moral issues that were affecting the church in Corinth, including sexual immorality and Christians suing one another in the courts. This was messy church. The work of rescue and restoration always is.

The Samaritan woman was not only in a mess morally, she was in a mess in her spiritual understanding, too. Because of her background as a Samaritan, she had all kinds of misinformation and misunderstandings regarding salvation. She was—as all of us are before God opens our eyes—spiritually blind. But Jesus was not put off by her blindness and confusion. Patiently he unravelled her misunderstandings and led her out of her confusion.

If you are to reach others for Christ, you will constantly be faced with the same spiritual blindness and ignorance. Sometimes we can find this frustrating and even infuriating. I remember spending a couple of hours with a friend talking to one young man. We answered his questions and explained the gospel as clearly as we could. At the end of this time he turned to me and in all seriousness said, 'So you do believe in God, then.' Helping people to understand the good news takes a lot of patience and a lot of prayer. Ultimately, only God can open the eyes of the blind; but he uses people like you and me in the process. The question is: are we willing to give ourselves to this challenging and often long-term work?

There are many barriers in people's understanding, especially in the increasingly secular West. Decades of atheistic teaching in our schools and anti-Christian bias in the media have helped to strengthen these barriers.

Understanding where people are coming from is a massive part of effective communication. Their thinking processes, presuppositions and past experiences will all affect how they hear what you are saying to them. Just as Jesus did with the woman of Samaria, we are going to have to understand and pick through these in order to clearly explain the gospel. Unlike Jesus, we don't usually have the advantage of divine knowledge of people, so it may take more time and will involve lots of listening as well as speaking.

If we are going to reach a lost world we need to be barrier-breakers and, if I can mix my metaphors, bridge-builders. It will mean stepping out of our comfort zones, challenging our prejudices and constantly changing. It's never easy to do this, but if we really care, we will do it.

Personal or group study: 1 Corinthians 9:19–23;10:31–33

1. *How does Paul describe his relationship to unsaved people and his motive for thinking this way (9:19, 23)?*
2. *What effect does this putting others first have on his behaviour (9:20–22)?*
3. *How might this pragmatic approach affect the way we behave?*
4. *How does 10:31–33 act as a check on going too far in this pragmatic approach?*

3 Opportunity: Seeing and seizing the opportunity

Jesus had a divine appointment with the woman at the well. It was not mere coincidence or chance that they met that day. In fact, her salvation had been planned even before Jacob had dug the well over a thousand years earlier. The Bible tells us we were chosen in him before the very foundation of the world (Eph. 1:4). Nothing happens by chance with God and he is constantly at work behind the scenes, ordering our circumstances to bring about his purposes in our lives. That is as true before our conversion as after.

I once heard an evangelist tell the following story. He was on his way to speak at a meeting when he passed two hitchhikers at the side of the road. He didn't stop. A few miles on, however, he felt that God was telling him to go back and give these two young men a lift. So he turned the car round, went back and picked them up. As they were travelling one of the men asked the evangelist if he was a Christian. 'Yes,' he happily replied, 'why do you ask?' At that point the young man turned to his companion and said, 'There you are: I told you so!' It turned out he had recently become a Christian, and his non-Christian friend with whom he was hitching had said, 'If there's a God, pray we will get a lift.' Not to be outdone by his friend, the new Christian had said: 'I will pray we get a lift from a real Christian!'

The story didn't end there. Part-way through the journey they stopped at a roadside cafe for something to eat. Over the meal they began to have a conversation about salvation. At one point the unconverted man turned to the evangelist and said, 'All you say is very convincing, but I have only ever met two real Christians: you and my friend here.' At that point the waiter, who was passing and had been listening in to the conversation, stopped, put out his hand and said, 'Meet the third!' Just chance? I don't believe so; God had an appointment with that young man that day.

When I look back I can think of key people and conversations that were part of my coming to faith. I am sure some of those people at the time thought little of what was said, but God was at work.

It is an exciting thing to think that any of us can play a part in that eternal plan of salvation for another person. When you start to think that way, it can change your attitude to your everyday life. The people you meet in the course of an ordinary day may well be people in whom God is already at work.

In John 4, a simple conversation about a point of common interest is turned into a deep conversation about spiritual need. There are many lessons we can learn from Jesus on how to turn the tables on a conversation and make it something of eternal significance that God can use.

CONTACT

The first thing to be said is that the conversation takes place at a point of contact that is very natural and non-threatening.

The well in the first century was a natural meeting place. Jesus begins by simply asking for a drink. If for a moment you take out of the equation the fact he is a Jewish man and she a Samaritan woman, a drink is a very natural thing to talk about at a well. A general principle in most evangelism is that making a friendly point of contact is the best way to start. People are far more likely to listen to you if they feel comfortable with you.

Where possible, longer-term relationships are best for creating a context in which to share our faith. That way, our lives can speak as well as our words. However, there are simply not enough Christians to reach everyone in this way, so what is sometimes referred to as 'cold contact' evangelism is also necessary if we are to reach this generation for Christ. This can be done in a myriad different ways. Gospel tracts or leaflets given out in the streets or a questionnaire from house to house can be used as the way to open the door of conversation. A friend of mine will always give a simple gospel explanation to any telephone salesperson who rings his home.

If we think about it, all of us come into regular contact with non-Christians every day. We visit many different 'wells'. It may be the work 'well', where we meet colleagues, or the home 'well', where we meet family and neighbours, or the leisure 'well', such as the gym. I am sure you could think of many non-Christians you regularly see at all these places. Try putting down the names of five people you meet regularly at one of your 'wells'. At the beginning of every week, pray that God would give you an opportunity to share something of the gospel message with them.

INITIATIVE

The next thing we see about this conversation is that Jesus takes the initiative. He introduces the subject of living water. He is intentional and proactive. So is the Samaritan woman when she returns to the town to tell the people what has happened to her, and then takes them to meet Jesus. It has been suggested that the average Christian's witnessing should only be *reactive*, just waiting for the subject to be raised and then responding to questions. Certainly we should be doing that; it is what Peter talks about in his first epistle.

> Always be prepared to give an answer to everyone who asks you to give the reason for the hope that you have. But do this with gentleness and respect, keeping a clear conscience, so that those who speak maliciously against your good behaviour in Christ may be ashamed of their slander (1 Peter 3:15).

Peter is saying that as we live consistent Christian lives, people will notice and begin to ask questions. We need to be ready to answer those questions with a clear explanation of what we believe. However, when you look at the book of Acts, for example, you will also see a lot of proactive witnessing by ordinary Christians who boldly took the initiative. In Acts 2 it wasn't just the apostle Peter who witnessed to the crowd, it was all of the 120 who were in the upper room. The crowd said in amazement, 'We hear them declaring the wonders of God in our own tongues!' (Acts 2:11).

Acts 11 tells us about the powerful witness of the believers who had left Jerusalem because of the persecution following the stoning of Stephen. It is interesting that there is no mention of the apostles, nor were these people specially gifted evangelists. They were just ordinary Christians taking every opportunity to tell others the gospel, and God honoured their witness. Yes, there are specially gifted evangelists and preachers whom God uses. They play a vital role in the outreach of the church, and we need more of them. However, although we can't all be gifted evangelists—nor should we try to be—we can all gossip the gospel.

CURIOSITY

The third practical thing we can learn from this master class in witnessing is the need for subtlety and sensitivity. Jesus doesn't just dive in. He first 'throws out some bait', like a fisherman tempting the fish with a juicy worm. He stimulates the woman's curiosity:

> Jesus answered her, 'If you knew the gift of God and who it is that asks you for a drink, you would have asked him and he would have given you living water' (John 4:10).

Sometimes, in our eagerness and anxiety, we blunder right in with a four-point sermon without thinking about the person to whom we are speaking. Jesus' approach is gentle and subtle. We can learn from this. We don't have to say everything all at once. Just a throwaway comment about how we enjoyed church on Sunday, or about something we are reading in a Christian book, or a Christian view of a current issue, might be enough to start a conversation. We don't have to bash the door down; just a gentle knock is often all it takes to get the door open a little.

When the woman responds with interest, Jesus takes her a step at a time. As the conversation progresses, so does her openness, and so does his directness. By the end, 'the penny is dropping':

> The woman said, 'I know that Messiah' (called Christ) 'is coming. When he comes, he will explain everything to us.' Then Jesus declared, 'I, the one speaking to you—I am he' (vv. 25–26).

Sometimes we have got to know when to end a conversation as well as when to start it. We need to pray for sensitivity to God's leading, and for his wisdom and discernment. He will give it.

DIFFICULT QUESTIONS

We can also learn from the way Jesus deals with the woman's question:

> 'Sir,' the woman said, 'I can see that you are a prophet. Our ancestors worshipped on this mountain, but you Jews claim that the place where we must worship is in Jerusalem.'
>
> 'Woman,' Jesus replied, 'believe me, a time is coming when you will worship the Father neither on this mountain nor in Jerusalem. You Samaritans worship what you do not know; we worship what we do know, for salvation is from the Jews. Yet a time is coming and has now come when the true worshippers will worship the Father in the Spirit and in truth, for they are the kind of worshippers the Father seeks. God is spirit, and his worshippers must worship in the Spirit and in truth' (vv. 19–24).

It is often the fear of an awkward question that puts many people off witnessing. If you honestly don't have a clue how to answer a question you've been asked, the best thing is simply to admit it. I know of one student who was converted after asking a Christian friend a difficult question to which she simply admitted she didn't have an answer. The honesty and humility of this Christian girl made a huge impact. If you find yourself in that situation, you can always offer to go and find out, and come back with an answer another time. There are many Christian books containing answers to difficult questions. You could even offer a copy of one.

Back in John, the conversation has reached a particularly difficult stage. Jesus has just asked the woman to go and call her husband, knowing full well that she is living with a man who is not her husband. It may be that this is her attempt to change the topic of conversation to a less uncomfortable one. Somebody once suggested that with every question you should work out the RH factor: is it a Real Hindrance or a Red Herring? Some questions may be better left to one side because they are not real problems and are going to lead nowhere, or, worse still, cause an argument.

The question the woman asks is at the heart of the controversy between the Jews and the Samaritans. The Jews, in line with God's command, worshipped at the temple in Jerusalem, but the Samaritans had built another temple on Mount Gerizim and worshipped there instead. Notice the way Jesus answers her question. First, he is honest and doesn't try to hide the truth: 'You Samaritans worship what you do not know; we worship what we do know, for salvation is from the Jews.' In other words, he is saying that the Samaritans are wrong and the Jews are right on this.

THE QUESTION BEHIND THE QUESTION

But he also answers the question behind the question: how can a person worship God? Jesus tells her that true worship comes from the heart. It is when our hearts are right with God that we truly worship. It is not an issue of geography but of reality. It's the heart reality that matters to God. That is something anyone can experience. Salvation may be from the Jews—Jesus was born a Jew—but it is not only for the Jews: it is for the whole world. Not only is it not about geography, it is also not about nationality. All of this is because of Jesus and the difference he is making. So Jesus answers her question, and also the question behind it. He keeps it from becoming a distraction from the real issue: her personal need to know God. 'Keep the main thing the main thing' is not a bad maxim when it comes to witnessing.

SOME SCENARIOS

Taking on board these principles, here are a few scenarios to illustrate how this might look in practice.

Scenario 1

Mike: I don't know how you can believe in God when there is so much suffering going on in the world.

Paul: To be honest, I don't have all the answers when it comes to suffering, but I've come to the position where there is enough I do understand about God's love to trust him for the things I don't yet understand.

Mike: Like what?

Paul: Well, I know that God has not remained distant from our suffering world but has come to live in the middle of it and has suffered with us. That is who I believe Jesus is: Jesus is God who came to live among humans as a human. He suffered emotionally and physically just as we do. And more

than that, he went to the cross and suffered for us. The Bible says it was because God loved the world that Jesus died for the world. He took on him the suffering we deserve for our guilt, so we could be forgiven.
Mike: What difference is that going to make to some poor family caught up in a war or a famine?
Paul: I have never been through anything like that, so what do I know? But plenty of Christians have, and many of them would say that knowing God loves them and is in control of their lives has given them the strength to face it. I have found that to be true in my own life too when things have gone wrong. Christians also know this life isn't going to last for ever, so they can look forward to a day when there will be no more suffering, when they are in heaven.

Scenario 2
Mike: You're not one of those homophobic Christians, are you?
Paul: I don't hate gays, if that's what you mean. You couldn't hate someone and follow Jesus. He said you should love everyone, even those who hate you.
Mike: So do you think it's OK to be gay, then?
Paul: Before I answer that one I think you have got to ask another question, and that is: how do you decide what is right and wrong? Is it down to popular opinion, or is it just your own personal preference that counts? As a Christian, I believe it's neither of those two options. I believe that the God who made us knows what is best for us and he has told us what is right and wrong. So when God says heterosexual relationships are his pattern for people, I know that ultimately that is for everyone's

good. That doesn't apply just to sexuality: it applies to all of life. I have found that, no matter how difficult it might be to follow God's definition of right and wrong, it is always the best thing to do. I also know that, although we all fail to do what is right, God still loves us and wants to forgive and help us to live life the way he intended.

Scenario 3

Mike: So what about all the other religions in the world: those who follow them are sincere in what they believe, so what makes you think you are right?

Paul: I don't doubt their sincerity, but sincerity isn't everything: you can be sincerely wrong. People used to sincerely believe the world was flat and you could fall off the edge, but that didn't make it true. In the end, you need some evidence that supports your belief.

Mike: So what's yours?

Paul: The best evidence is Jesus himself. He said, 'I am the way and the truth and the life. No one comes to the Father except through me.' That was a personal and exclusive claim to be the only way to God.

Mike: That's very bigoted, isn't it?

Paul: Well, it would be if I said it, but Jesus has the authority to make that claim because he is God. He proved that he was God by doing what only God can do: he rose from the dead.

Mike: Where's the proof for that?

Paul: There's loads of evidence, like the empty tomb, the witnesses who saw him alive, and the change Jesus made to so many lives. I've got a really good book written by a guy who didn't believe it was true until he looked at the evidence—I could lend you a copy if you want.

As you visit your 'wells' each day, go with an expectant attitude. Have your spiritual antennae up, prayerfully seeking opportunities to share the message of life with thirsty people who need Jesus. Sensitively, but boldly, take those opportunities and see what God does through you. You may be surprised by who is waiting at your well.

Personal or group study: Acts 8:26–40

1. *How does Philip's sensitivity to God's leading make his witnessing so much more effective (vv. 26–27, 29)?*
2. *How does this incident illustrate our part and God's part in the work of evangelism?*
3. *How does this story illustrate the principle of starting where people are, and the need to therefore listen before we speak (vv. 30–35)?*
4. *How does this passage encourage us to be ready for opportunities to witness in our everyday lives?*

4 Process: Sowing and reaping

I've never been green-fingered; I can kill most plants. Although I am not very good in the garden, I do know that the only things that grow without any work are weeds. Everything else takes time and effort if you want to reap the rewards. There is a process involved in growing things, and that process involves time and work. That is especially true if you want to grow crops. Sowing comes first; then the plants must be nurtured; and finally the harvest needs gathering in.

Jesus uses the analogy of agriculture in John 4 when he wants to teach his disciples about witnessing:

> Don't you have a saying, 'It's still four months until harvest'? I tell you, open your eyes and look at the fields! They are ripe for harvest. Even now the one who reaps draws a wage and harvests a crop for eternal life, so that the sower and the reaper may be glad together. Thus the saying 'One sows and another reaps' is true. I sent you to reap what you have not worked for. Others have done the hard work, and you have reaped the benefits of their labour (John 4:35–38).

Jesus is teaching that, just as there is a process involved in the physical harvest, so it is with the spiritual harvest. It is important to understand this process in order to avoid discouragement. Before there can be reaping, there must be sowing. This Samaritan woman became a believer on the very day she met Christ by the well, as did many in the town of Sychar, but Jesus implies that the seed had already been sown in their lives. It was only because others had done this sowing work that the harvest could be reaped on this occasion. Exactly what this sowing was we do not know; it may just have been a knowledge of the scriptural promises of the coming Messiah. However it happened, the seeds had been sown, and now they had germinated, producing a crop to eternal life.

When someone comes to faith it is the climax of a journey, the final link in a chain. Many things may have led up to that moment. Seeds have been sown in that person's life over a period of time. These seeds may be life experiences, books or tracts they have read, people they have met, conversations they have had or meetings they have attended. As Jesus points out, the person who does the sowing may not be the same person who does the reaping, but both are essential if there is to be a harvest.

We all want the job of harvesting. There is a great thrill in being the person God uses to lead someone in that moment of commitment. But remember: you can only reap where others have sown. This means we need faithful sowers of gospel seed. It also means we shouldn't get discouraged when we don't see the fruits of our labours. Sometimes the seed can lie dormant for many years before it springs into life. Sowing work is not wasted work.

While conducting a university mission once, I was staying in the house of a pastor, and at the breakfast table I met his lodger, a young man in his late twenties. He looked at me and exclaimed, 'You're the milk-bottle man!' At first I thought he had me mixed up with the milkman, but actually he was referring to a story I had told twenty years previously in a primary-school assembly in his home town. The story of the milk bottle had been part of my testimony that I had shared that day with the children. I hadn't met him since, but that ten-minute talk had stayed with him for twenty years. You could have knocked me down with a feather! He hadn't yet trusted Christ but was now thinking seriously about doing so. You never know what God is going to do with the seed you sow.

On another occasion, at the end of a meeting at which I had spoken, a man approached me, put out his hand and uttered those dreaded words, 'Do you remember me?' I had to confess that I didn't. It turned out we were on the same course at university and had sat next to each other in lectures fifteen years earlier. As he spoke, I began to realize who he was. He had been a hardened atheist who had been utterly impervious to my attempts at witnessing. And here he was, smiling from ear to ear, telling me he was now a Christian. He met other Christians after university and they had led him to Christ. What an encouragement to know that those difficult conversations in the lecture theatre, or at that school assembly, had been part of what God had used to bring about a harvest to eternal life! Never underestimate the power of gospel seed sown in an individual. We will have to wait till heaven to see the full extent of the harvest of souls that God has brought about through the seed we have sown. I suspect we are in for many joyful surprises.

There may be times when we will predominantly be sowing. For example, in Western Europe in the past, evangelists were able to do a lot of reaping because a lot of sowing had already been done. There was much more exposure to Christian teaching in schools and many more were brought up to attend church, especially as children. Today, in our increasingly secular world where there is great ignorance of the Bible and little exposure to the gospel, more sowing of the seed may need to be done in comparison with harvesting.

PRODUCTIVE AND UNPRODUCTIVE SOIL

In Mark 4 Jesus tells three parables about sowing seeds. The first, the Parable of the Sower (vv. 1–20), reminds us that some seed may be unproductive, falling on unsuitable ground, but there will be some that falls on good ground and produces a harvest. The problem is not with the sower or the seed, but with the soil. We shouldn't be surprised or discouraged when people don't respond with a lasting commitment to Christ. Jesus tells us to expect this. There will always have to be more sowing than harvesting, as some seed will be lost. Our job is to plant as much seed as possible, in as many places as possible, because we don't know what the ground is like. Obviously, the more seed we sow, the better the chances that it will land on good ground. The parable encourages us to keep sowing, because there will always be some good soil that will produce lasting results.

PATIENCE NEEDED

The second parable in Mark 4, the Parable of the Growing Seed (vv. 26–29), teaches us that patience is needed; it takes time for the seed to grow.

Remember that it's a process. The parable also reminds us that our job is to plant and sow, while it is God's job to make the seed grow. Paul reminds the Corinthians of this in his first letter to them:

> I planted the seed, Apollos watered it, but God has been making it grow (1 Cor. 3:6).

Be faithful in doing your part, and God will do his.

SMALL BEGINNINGS PRODUCE BIG RESULTS

The third parable, the Parable of the Mustard Seed (vv. 30–32), shows us that, although, like the mustard seed, the work of God may have small beginnings and seem insignificant, it will have big results.

Anthony Ashley Cooper, 7th Earl of Shaftesbury, was perhaps the greatest social reformer of the nineteenth century in England. He was neglected by his own father and mother and was largely brought up by Maria Mills, an old family servant. Maria, a Christian, taught the young earl to love the Scriptures, and it was through her influence that Shaftesbury came to trust Christ as a boy. When he grew up, he became a Member of Parliament and began his campaign to drive through the reforms that helped improve the lives of millions of England's poor. Shaftesbury always attributed his social concern to his Christian faith. It was the witness of that simple girl, Maria, that God used to affect the lives of millions. Small seeds of the kingdom planted in the heart of that young boy had produced something huge.

Another example of this principle can be seen in the story of one of the greatest evangelists of the nineteenth century, D. L. Moody. As a young man Moody attended a Sunday school class in the town of Boston, USA. One day his Sunday school teacher, Edward Kimble, went to see Moody in the shoe shop where he worked. Kimble had become deeply concerned about Moody's spiritual state, and there at the back of the shoe shop he pleaded with him to trust Christ, which he did. Moody went on to preach the gospel to huge crowds around the world, with hundreds of thousands coming to faith. It all began with that small seed planted in the heart of that young man by a faithful Sunday school teacher.

A friend of mine was converted through reading half of John 3:16 that had been printed on the back of a bus ticket. Never underestimate the power of gospel seed planted in a life. What seems small and insignificant can have massive consequences.

THREE POWERFUL WITNESSES

There are good reasons for us to be very confident of positive results as we sow gospel seed. When we witness to someone we are not alone: there are a number of powerful witnesses that join us.

First, there is the witness of that person's spirit. There are things that everyone, even an atheist, knows deep down to be true. Paul tells us in Romans that all people know in their heart of hearts that there is a God:

> The wrath of God is being revealed from heaven against all the godlessness and wickedness of people, who suppress the truth by their wickedness, since what may be known about God is plain to them, because God has made it plain to them. For since the creation of the world God's invisible qualities—his eternal power and divine nature—have been clearly seen, being understood from what has been made, so that people are without excuse (Rom. 1:18–20).

Paul says that people see the evidence for God in creation, but choose to suppress that truth. The idea is of pushing down on something that is exerting a constant pressure in the opposite direction. That is what people who deny the existence of God are doing: they are fighting against something they know to be true. The problem of unbelief is at root not intellectual: it is moral and spiritual. One atheist very honestly said to me, 'I accept chance evolution because the alternative is special creation, which I cannot accept.'

Paul also teaches us that, deep down, people know they have sinned:

> Indeed, when Gentiles, who do not have the law, do by nature things required by the law, they are a law for themselves, even though they do not have the law. They show that the requirements of the law are written on their hearts, their consciences also bearing witness, and their thoughts sometimes accusing them and at other times even defending them (Rom. 2:14–15).

He says that even those who know nothing of God's standards of right and wrong, written in the Bible, know the difference because they have a God-given conscience. That inner voice is constantly witnessing to them about their sin. This means that when we talk about sin and guilt, a voice within them says, 'Yes, that is true.' People may—and do—choose to ignore or suppress that voice, but it is still there.

Finally, Paul tells us that people also know they will face God in judgement:

> Just as they did not think it worth while to retain the knowledge of God, so God gave them over to a depraved mind, so that they do what ought not to be done … Although they know God's righteous decree that those who do such things deserve death,

> they not only continue to do these very things but also approve of those who practise them (Rom. 1:28, 32).

One man said, 'It's not that I fear there is nothing after death, but that I fear there is something.' In one sense, part of our job as witnesses is to affirm what people already know. We are simply reminding them of what deep down they know is true.

The second powerful witness that joins us in our evangelism is the witness of the Scriptures. It is always important to remember that our authority comes from God's Word, and that Word is authoritative. It has a power of its own. That is why I always recommend getting people to look at the Bible with you. Paul reminds Timothy of the power Scripture had in his life when he was a boy:

> You know … how from infancy you have known the Holy Scriptures, which are able to make you wise for salvation through faith in Christ Jesus (2 Tim. 3:14–15).

The Bible gets to people in a way that our own words cannot. Hebrews 4 reminds us of this:

> For the word of God is alive and active. Sharper than any double-edged sword, it penetrates even to dividing soul and spirit, joints and marrow; it judges the thoughts and attitudes of the heart. Nothing in all creation is hidden from God's sight. Everything is uncovered and laid bare before the eyes of him to whom we must give account (Heb. 4:12–13).

Finally, as we witness, so too does the Holy Spirit. God's Spirit is at work convicting and convincing people of what we are saying. Ultimately it is his secret work that is going to bring lasting results. Without him, people would never come to faith, but when he works, anyone can be saved. When Jesus tells his disciples they will be his witnesses, he encourages them by pointing to the work of the coming Spirit:

> I will send him [the Advocate] to you. When he comes, he will prove the world to be in the wrong about sin and righteousness and judgment (John 16:7–8).

The Holy Spirit reveals to people their need of forgiveness because of sin and judgement, and reveals the one who can bring that forgiveness: Jesus.

So we are not alone in witnessing: we have great and powerful forces at work on our side. The person's spirit, the Scriptures and the Spirit of God are working with us as we share the gospel.

LEADING A PERSON TO CHRIST

It may be that God uses you to be the harvester, the person who leads someone in that final act of trusting Christ. Here are some simple dos and don'ts if you find yourself in that privileged position:

- Do make sure that there is a clear understanding of what the gospel is (more of this in Chapter 5). Using a simple gospel outline such as 'Two Ways to Live' or 'The Bridge to Life' can be useful (see Chapter 6 for more about these). Ask questions to discover the clarity of this understanding. Give the person opportunity to ask questions too.
- Do explain the cost of following Christ. That involves a clear understanding of repentance and a changed life,

as well as of the possibility of persecution or rejection by others.

- Do use Scripture verses for what you say. Always have a pocket New Testament to hand so you can take the person to helpful verses.
- Do ask the person if he or she would like to pray with you there and then. You might like to offer a written prayer for the person's use, but I feel it is better for people to put their prayers into their own words.
- Don't be pushy. Always give the person the option of going away to think about it and pray on his or her own.
- Do explain the importance of prayer, Bible reading and fellowship. Introduce the person to a good church if he or she doesn't already attend one. Give the person some good daily Bible notes and a Bible if he or she doesn't have one. Encourage the person to start a daily devotion time.
- Do encourage the person to tell someone about what he or she has done. This helps new believers to begin verbalizing their faith and seal the commitment they have made.
- Do finish by praying for the person.
- Do give the person your phone number or email address, and encourage him or her to keep in touch regularly to discuss how things are going.

5 Message: What is the gospel?

The gospel is good news, but news, by definition, is only news if it is told. The gospel needs to be put into words; it's not enough just to live it out. News also needs to be clear and understood. It has been said that with modern means of communication we can get an idea around the world in a split second, but it sometimes takes years for it to get through a quarter of an inch of human skull. It is important to recognize from the start that ultimately it is only God's Spirit who can give that real understanding. However, we have a responsibility to work at making the message as clear as possible.

JESUS IS THE GOSPEL

At the heart of the gospel is not a philosophy of life, but life through a person. That person is Jesus. The life he brings is spiritual life. That is the truth that the Samaritan woman came to understand. It was that revelation that brought salvation to her that day. John tells us at the end of his Gospel that he wrote his book so that others also would find this life through believing in Jesus:

> Jesus performed many other signs in the presence of his disciples, which are not written in this book. But these are written that you may believe that Jesus is the Messiah, the Son of God, and that by believing you may have life in his name (John 20:30–31).

Notice it is not some vague belief in Jesus that brings life;

life comes by believing that Jesus is 'the Messiah, the Son of God'. We haven't begun to understand what the gospel is until we have understood who Jesus is. In the course of the conversation the Samaritan woman's understanding of Jesus develops. First she just sees him as a Jewish man. Of course, Jesus was a real man of history. The British writer H. G. Wells once said,

> I am a historian, I am not a believer, but I must confess as a historian that this penniless preacher from Nazareth is irrevocably the very centre of history. Jesus Christ is easily the most dominant figure in all history. Christ is the most unique person of history. No man can write a history of the human race without giving first and foremost place to the penniless teacher of Nazareth.

There is a wealth of historical evidence, both biblical and secular, that supports the historicity of Jesus. But Jesus was so much more than just a Jewish man, and the Samaritan woman begins to see that. Next she comes to the conclusion that he is a prophet. All that he tells her, especially of her own life, convinces her of that. Many are happy to call Jesus a prophet or teacher. Ghandi once famously said, 'Jesus was one of the mightiest teachers that ever lived.' But Jesus doesn't accept merely the title of prophet or teacher. He plainly declares to the woman that he is the Messiah:

> The woman said, 'I know that Messiah' (called Christ) 'is coming. When he comes, he will explain everything to us.' Then Jesus declared, 'I, the one speaking to you—I am he' (John 4:25–26).

The title Messiah means 'God's anointed'. In the Old Testament, kings were anointed, but it was foretold that one would come who would be God's King. Jesus is claiming to be that unique person. What he literally says to the woman is, 'I who speak to you, *I am*.' Jesus is deliberately taking to himself the sacred name of God. It was the name that God revealed to Moses. Jesus is making a remarkable statement about his true identity: he is God.

Any explanation of the gospel should clearly explain who Christ is. Some have said that it is better to start a gospel explanation with God the Father rather than with Jesus. However, although that approach has its merits, I don't think it is essential. Jesus reveals the Father to us, and that is why he came, as John tells us at the start of his Gospel:

> No one has ever seen God, but the one and only Son, who is himself God and is in the closest relationship with the Father, has made him known (John 1:18).

In a very sceptical world where people want evidence and proof, what greater evidence of God is there than Jesus? Actually, it could be argued that, when explaining the gospel, there is no better place to start than with Jesus.

HUMAN NEED

The gospel, then, is primarily about the person of Jesus. The gospel is also about human need. It is that need that Jesus fulfils. Jesus talks to this woman about her craving for life. That is something universal. But, says Jesus, it is essential to understand what that life really is and where it comes from. So much of what counts as life is mere existence. We eat, we sleep, we buy possessions and form relationships, but real living has another dimension to it. Prince Charles once said, 'There remains deep in the soul (dare I mention that word?!) of mankind a persistent and unconscious anxiety that something is missing—some vital ingredient that makes life truly worth living.'[1] Jesus wants that woman to see that the missing ingredient is the spiritual life that only he can give. The actor Jim Carey is reported to have said, 'Everyone should get the chance to be rich and famous and do all the things they have dreamed of doing, so they can realize it's not the answer.'

Sometimes, to begin, as Jesus does, with our felt sense of need for fulfilment is a good way into a conversation. It stirs up some of the big questions of life, its meaning and purpose. Notice that Jesus also introduces the idea of eternity into the equation:

> Jesus answered, 'Everyone who drinks this water will be thirsty again, but whoever drinks the water I give them will never thirst. Indeed, the water I give them will become in them a spring of water welling up to eternal life' (vv. 13–14).

ETERNAL LIFE

It's not just about the here and now. Life here is temporary. Jesus raises the great question of life beyond the grave. The illustration of water is a good one, as water not only quenches our thirst but also preserves our life. You can live without food for weeks, but you will survive only for a few days without water. Water is not a luxury, it's a necessity without which we die. This life that Christ offers is equally a matter of life and death: eternal life or eternal death. It's a question not just of why we are here, but of where we are going. The Bible says that God put eternity in our hearts. Deep down, we know that this life isn't all there is. The gospel actually has a future focus to it. It is about eternal life. Any explanation of the gospel that doesn't share that focus is also inadequate.

THE 'S' WORD

We now come to the tricky part of a faithful gospel explanation. Jesus deals with the woman's moral failure, her sin. He asks the woman to call her husband, knowing full well that she has had five, and that now she is living with a man outside of marriage. It's not that Jesus is trying to humiliate her or deny that she has been deeply hurt by her experiences; rather, he wants her to face up to her sinful behaviour. She may have been a victim of others' behaviour and attitudes, but she is not an innocent victim. She has to face up to her own responsibility too. This is something we all find difficult, but we must all do it if we want to be saved. People are very good at finding excuses for their sin rather than own up to it. I came across the following song by Anna Russell which expresses this desire to get ourselves off the hook:

I went to my psychiatrist to be psychoanalysed
To find out why I killed the cat and blackened my husband's eyes.
He laid me on a downy couch to see what he could find,
And here is what he dredged up from my subconscious mind:
When I was one, my mummy hid my dolly in a trunk,
And so it follows naturally that I am always drunk.
When I was two, I saw my father kiss the maid one day,
And that is why I suffer now from kleptomania.
At three, I had the feeling of ambivalence towards my brothers,
And so it follows naturally I poison all my lovers.
But I am happy; now I've learned the lesson this has taught;
That everything I do that's wrong is someone else's fault.

People use many expressions to try to minimize or excuse sin. We call it weakness, failing to fulfil your potential, low self-esteem or sickness. All these terms seek to redefine the concept of sin. In all these definitions the idea of our personal moral responsibility before God has been totally airbrushed out. One man said, 'Evil has gone from being sin, defined theologically (to do with God), to crime, defined legally (to do with its effect on society), to sickness, defined psychologically (to do with what it does to me).'

The Bible is not saying that we are all as bad as we could be, but rather that none of us is as good as we should be. As Paul says in Romans 3:23, 'All fall short of the glory of God.' A good illustration of this is to imagine we were to go on a trip to the Empire State Building in New York. Once there, we all have to choose a floor that represents how good or bad we think we are. I suspect most of us would choose a floor somewhere in the middle. We wouldn't put ourselves in the basement with Hitler, but neither would we put ourselves on the viewing platform at the very top. But where do you think God's standard of goodness would be? The answer is: the moon. In other words, it doesn't matter who we are: we have all fallen a million miles short of God's standard.

It is also important to get across that sin is not just a moral failure to live up to God's standards, it is a heart attitude towards God himself. It is refusing to acknowledge God as the supreme authority in our lives, a declaration of independence from God. It is saying that I am in charge of my life and I can live it without submitting to God. Sin is essentially rebellion.

This rejection of God shows itself in seeking satisfaction and significance in everything except God. When, in the

Old Testament, God spoke to the nation of Israel through Jeremiah, he said:

My people have committed two sins:
They have forsaken me,
  the spring of living water,
and have dug their own cisterns,
  broken cisterns that cannot hold water (Jer. 2:13).

The nation of Israel had turned from the true and living God to idols. They had sought life in those idols and not in God. Of course, they had been utterly frustrated and disappointed, as the life they sought could only be found in God. This God-replacement strategy is always at the heart of sin.

Jesus and Jeremiah both use the imagery of water and a well to show how only a relationship with God can bring true fulfilment and purpose. For this Samaritan woman, her failed relationships had been her 'broken cistern'. She had discovered the disappointment and damage caused by the sin of 'God replacement'.

As we try to explain sin we need to get to this root cause of sin. We need to expose the broken wells that we have dug looking for life everywhere except in God: in sex, status, possessions, family, just to name a few.

JUDGEMENT

God is just, and his justice demands that our sin be punished. The punishment is eternal separation from God. Unless we explain our sin and God's judgement of it, our message will always be a take-it or leave-it one. If the message is merely, 'Come to Jesus and you will be fulfilled', it is an incomplete and inadequate gospel. People can justifiably reply, 'I already feel fulfilled; why do I need Jesus?' Yes, the gospel is about fulfilment, but it is also about forgiveness. We need forgiveness because we have offended a holy God by our sin. That sin will rob us of life now and in eternity. Until we see that, we haven't properly understood the message. So it's not until a person has understood the bad news that he or she will understand the good news.

I am not a good flyer; I get nervous. On the occasions I have to fly, something always happens that makes me even more nervous. Once in my seat, the flight staff make an announcement. It's the instructions about what to do in an emergency. I've noticed that on most flights I'm the only passenger that takes any notice. While the exit lights that appear on the floor are being demonstrated, people are looking out of the window. While the life jacket is being shown, others are settling down for a snooze. I know it's sad, but I hang on to every word. I scrutinize the laminated sheet of safety diagrams kept in the pocket on the back of the seat in front of me. Nobody else seems interested. However, I guarantee that if, mid-flight, the pilot were to announce that the plane was in trouble and we had to make an emergency landing, everybody would suddenly be very interested in those emergency instructions. They would suddenly become the most important information on the plane.

Why are so many people apathetic about the gospel message? It is partly because they think it doesn't matter, that they don't really need it. But the truth is that they desperately need Jesus to save them. Without him, they are lost for ever. Their sin will separate them from God in this life and in the next. As hard as we might find it to talk about sin and God's judgement, if we love people, we must do so. It is cruel and unloving *not* to warn people. We mustn't do it in a self-righteous way, as if it's just their problem. It should be clear by the way we talk that we are no different from them.

THE CROSS

Then we need to explain what Jesus did to deal with our sin and make his forgiveness possible: the cross. Although Jesus doesn't mention his death to the woman at the well, it is clear as we read the Gospel of John that that is the focus of Christ's saving mission. In fact, about a third of John's Gospel covers the last week of his life. His death is the very heart of the gospel message. No gospel explanation is complete or adequate without a clear explanation of the work of the cross. The cross is about two big ideas: substitution and atonement. Substitution means that Christ took our place at the cross. We, the guilty, deserved to die, but he, the innocent one, died in our stead. The idea behind atonement is that Christ bore the punishment that we deserved. God poured out his righteous anger, which should have been directed against us, on Jesus. Because Christ took that punishment, we don't have to. We can be forgiven and made right with God. We find life through Christ's death.

It is important also to talk about the resurrection. Some gospel explanations leave Jesus dead, but he is not. He rose, showing that he has conquered death. He's alive; and just as the woman found life by hearing the message and meeting Christ, so we both hear the message and, by his Spirit, meet the living Christ.

REPENTANCE AND FAITH

Finally, we need to talk about repentance and faith. This is something that is often missing from gospel explanations. Repentance means turning from our old way of life to a new one lived for God. It means a leaving and a following: leaving sin and following Christ. Repentance is a key part of how we need to respond to the gospel and receive new life. Faith, or trust, is the other side of the coin of our response. We must turn from our sin to trust in, and submit to, Christ as boss of our lives.

RELATIONSHIP

The good news of the Christian message is that we can have a personal relationship with God. It is this that makes real Christianity more than just a religion. It is not a set of rites and rituals, rules and regulations, but a relationship. It is more than just something to be believed: it is someone to experience. A relationship is dynamic, not static. So when we share the gospel, we need to explain that becoming a Christian is just the beginning of this relationship, and that the relationship will grow and deepen as we get to know God better.

TELLING IT LIKE IT IS

We are to be heralds of the gospel. That is the idea behind one of the Greek words that is translated 'to preach' in our Bibles. In the first century the herald would make important public proclamations. A crowd would gather, and the herald's job was accurately and clearly to tell everyone listening the message he had been sent to deliver. The herald was not at liberty to edit or amend the message; it had to be delivered just as it had been given to him. As heralds of the gospel, we too must deliver that message accurately and clearly. We cannot edit out bits that we, or our audience, don't like. There is an offence in the gospel message. Paul tells us that while it will be a savour of life to some, it will be a savour of death to others. To some, the message of sin, judgement, the cross and the need for repentance will be like a bad smell. The temptation is always to try to make the message attractive to everyone, by cutting out the difficult or challenging bits. But we are not at liberty to do that. It is God's gospel, not ours. We are called upon to be faithful heralds. It is worth remembering, however, that we don't have to explain all of the message all at once. It may be that different aspects will be covered over the course of many conversations over a long period of time. There is a lot to take in, especially if someone has never really heard it before, so don't overload. Letting someone go away and think about one aspect is not a bad thing.

JARGON-FREE ZONE

It's really important when explaining the gospel that you try to put yourself in the listener's shoes. Try to use language that is familiar and understandable to that person. Don't use jargon or long theological terms. Words like 'salvation', 'redeemed' and 'justified' may mean a lot to you, but they are often incomprehensible to the average non-Christian. Keep it as simple as possible. Often, as Christians, we forget what it was like before we were converted. What may seem like a very basic concept can be very confusing to someone who is hearing it for the first time, so make your gospel conversation a jargon-free zone.

Personal or group study: Romans 3:21–26

1. *How do verses 22b and 23 show that the gospel is a universal message that all need to hear?*
2. *What is God's universal solution to that need (vv. 24–25a)?*
3. *Why is it important that we tell people the truth about their sinfulness?*
4. *Why did Jesus need to die in order that we might be forgiven (v. 26)?*
5. *What is the response that God wants to the gospel (vv. 22, 25–26)?*

Note

1 'A Speech by HRH The Prince of Wales at the Inauguration of The Prince of Wales's Institute of Architecture, St James's Palace, London', published on 30 January 1992, http://www.princeofwales.gov.uk/media/speeches/speech-hrh-the-prince-of-wales-the-inauguration-of-the-prince-of-waless-institute-of; accessed 26 August 2016.

6 Pictures: Using illustrations as a way to communicate the gospel

It has been said that 'the mind is not a debating chamber; it is a picture gallery'. I'm not sure I agree with the first half of that quote, but the second part is spot on. If you look at how God speaks to us in his Word, he often uses pictures to get a point across.

Jesus used the water in the well as an illustration when he spoke with the Samaritan woman. The water in the well was a picture of the spiritual life he was offering. The spring supplying the well with water is likened to the inexhaustible eternal life that Jesus would give her. Using imagery to teach spiritual truths is something Jesus often did. The parables are simple, everyday stories that became powerful illustrations of what Jesus was teaching.

The writers of the New Testament letters, such as Paul or James, also often use imagery as a teaching tool. Look, for example, at James 3. In just the first twelve verses, James uses seven different illustrations to teach about the power of the tongue. In the letter of Jude, six different images are used in just two sentences (vv. 12–13). If you add to that the

Old Testament stories Jude uses as illustrations, that makes sixteen in just this one short letter.

In the Old Testament, too, we find many different uses of illustrations to make a point. The tabernacle itself was one giant visual aid to show how sinful people could come to a holy God—ultimately pointing to Jesus. When the prophet Nathan confronts King David with his sin of adultery with Bathsheba (2 Sam. 12), he does so by using an illustration. He tells the simple story of a rich man who stole a poor man's only lamb so he could make a meal for a visitor. It is a powerful picture of what David has done in taking another man's wife.

Illustrations are effective for a number of reasons. They make difficult things easier to understand. Someone has compared them to windows in a building: they 'let in light'. They can make something memorable: we remember stories or images for a long time. Illustrations also help to get or hold attention. Illustrations can stir powerful emotions. Nathan's story of the stolen lamb is a classic example. When David heard about the injustice of what the rich man had done, he was incensed, and then deeply convicted when he realized he was that man.

MAKING THE CONNECTION

Illustrations can also connect with the world people live in and are familiar with. When I gave a talk at one university mission, I began by quoting the suicide note of Kurt Cobain, the lead singer with the rock group Nirvana. A student came up to me directly afterwards to tell me she had been talking about the death of Kurt Cobain with a friend on the way to the meeting. Hearing it spoken about in the talk had really challenged her, and she trusted the Lord that very night.

I really can't understand why some preachers don't use illustrations. But it's not just a good principle for preachers: it's great for anyone trying to communicate the gospel. There are many great gospel illustrations that can be used, and I am always on the lookout for new ones. They may come out of your own experience—personal illustrations can be especially effective. But they can just as easily be news items or stories found on the Internet. I have often found newspapers to be a good source. I once read the story of a young pregnant mum who was diagnosed with cancer and told by the surgeons that they could save either her or her unborn child. The article spoke of the incredible decision she made to forgo treatment so her child could live. I have used that story to illustrate the incredible decision Jesus made to die on the cross for us. Like the young mother, he could have saved himself; but if he had done so, we would have to die. Out of love he chose to die so that we can live. Again, I once saw a poster for the British Heart Foundation with a picture of a ribcage and the slogan, 'Inside this cage lurks Britain's biggest killer'. I have used that to talk about the problem of sin in our hearts. If you hear a good illustration in a sermon or read one in a book, use it yourself. Films can also be a great source of illustrations.

Visual gospel explanations can be especially helpful. I have often used 'The Bridge to Life',[1] something you can easily draw on a notepad or even a napkin. 'Two Ways to Live'[2] is also a good one, although slightly more complicated to draw. You can get both of these already drawn for you in booklet form.[3] Why not carry some copies with you, in case the opportunity to use them arises.

Notes

1 'The Bridge to Life', by the Navigators, https://www.navigators.org/Tools/Evangelism%20Resources/Tools/The%20Bridge%20to%20Life.

2 'Two Ways to Live', http://www.matthiasmedia.com.au/2wtl/.

3 'The Bridge to Life' is published by NavPress; 'Two Ways to Live' is published by Matthias Media.

7 Testimony: The power of a personal story

Many of the Samaritans from that town believed in him because of the woman's testimony, 'He told me everything I've ever done' (John 4:39).

It is the woman's story—of how she met Jesus and the conversation that changed her life—which makes such an impact on the people of the town. Personal stories are powerful things. The apostle Paul uses his testimony on a number of occasions in the book of Acts. In fact, on six separate occasions between his third missionary journey and his trip to Rome he stood before different audiences, many of them hostile, and told the story of his conversion (Acts 22–26). Paul knew the power of a testimony.

Every Christian has a testimony. The story of your journey to faith is something that is unique to you, and God can use it. Often a personal testimony is the thing that God uses to stop people in their tracks and start them thinking about the gospel. People are interested in other people's lives. The TV soap operas and fly-on-the-wall documentaries demonstrate how curious we are about each other. There are many positive things about sharing your testimony. Your personal story is a non-threatening way to introduce your faith. You are talking about yourself and not others, so your audience feels less under the spotlight. You can, in fact, say many things through your own experience which it might initially be difficult to say directly.

Your testimony is your experience, so it is very hard for others to argue with. A testimony is also a great way of breaking down some of the bad stereotypes people have of Christians. You can show that Christians live normal lives, and struggle with the same things as everyone else.

A testimony also shows the relevance of the gospel to ordinary people. It's not a theoretical message for theologians in ivory towers. Your testimony is evidence that there is a God and that Christianity really works. Your testimony is a powerful tool that God has given you to get the gospel to others, so learn to use it.

BE PREPARED

So how do you go about sharing your testimony? Spend some time in thought and preparation. It is worth writing down your story to get the facts clear in your own mind. It doesn't have to be a 500-page biography: just one side of A4 will do. This will also help you to be able to share your story concisely, without rambling or getting distracted by irrelevancies. Think about your life before you met the Lord. What was going on in the period leading up to your conversion? What problems or needs were you experiencing at the time? How did your life change afterwards?

A three-point approach can be helpful in structuring your story:

- *What you were*. Simply describe what your life was like before you became a Christian. What did you think about God, faith or church? Were you searching? What really filled your life? What were your priorities?

- *What happened.* Simply talk about the events and circumstances that caused you to consider trusting Christ. What was happening at the time? What was it about the gospel that particularly struck you? Talk about the questions you asked and how you found the answers, and the people or issues that influenced your decision. Explain, without preaching a long sermon, what it is you have come to believe. Make it clear exactly what you did. If there was a moment when you prayed, describe it and how you felt.
- *What you are now.* How has your life changed? How has God's forgiveness affected you? How have your thoughts, attitudes and emotions changed? How has your lifestyle changed? How is Christ meeting your needs, and what does a relationship with him mean to you now?

Be specific: people are interested in details; they make your story tangible and real. Be honest. Don't exaggerate for effect. You may feel that a story of conversion from a life of crime and drug addiction would be far more powerful, but actually the story of an ordinary person coming to faith may connect far better with most people, who have also lived ordinary lives. The simple truth of what God has done in your life is what he will use. Don't gloss over your struggles or failures as a Christian. Remember that the gospel is all about God's grace, so it is good when people see that we are forgiven sinners, not super-saints.

Avoid jargon phrases that are meaningless to non-

Christians, such as ‘I asked Jesus into my heart’. It might be much better to say, ‘I prayed, asking Jesus to take control of my life.’ Try to put things in the everyday language that everybody uses. Keep things as simple as you can. Some things that take a huge amount of background explanation may be best left out. Stick to the main points.

Finally, make sure all the glory goes to God and not to you. It is the story of his work of grace in you, and that should be the thought you leave with people.

A testimony alone is not enough; it should at some point be followed by a clear, biblical explanation of the gospel. It is important that people see where the final authority for our message lies. That authority is with God and his Word, and not just our experience. The gospel is not true because it works; it works because it’s true. Truth always comes before experience. Our experience can, however, illuminate and illustrate the truth.

Personal or group study: Acts 26:1–29

1. *How does Paul describe his life before he became a Christian, and how does this show his honesty (vv. 4–11)?*
2. *What can we learn from the way Paul describes his conversion experience (vv. 12–18)?*
3. *How does Paul describe his post-conversion life, and how does this summarize an important aspect of what it means to be a Christian (v. 19)?*
4. *How does Paul end his testimony (v. 29)?*

8 Urgency: Still four months?

On 15 April 1912 the SS *Titanic* plunged 13,000 feet to the bottom of the Atlantic. It was one of the worst maritime disasters in history. One of the reasons for the great loss of life was the fact that there were only enough lifeboats for half the passengers and crew. The other tragedy is that many of those lifeboats were only partially filled. Most of the passengers ended up struggling in the icy seas while those in the boats waited a safe distance away. They could hear the cries of the drowning people, but they would not go back for fear of a crush from those seeking rescue. Only one lifeboat returned: lifeboat no. 14. It chased the cries in the darkness, seeking and saving a precious few.

It is hard to imagine what it must have been like that night. What would I have done had I been in one of those half-empty boats? Would I have taken the risk of going back to save others? I guess we all like to think we would have done so, but it is something we will never know for sure. There is something we do know, however, and that is whether we are seeking to rescue spiritually lost people. If you're a Christian, you are in the lifeboat: you have been saved. The question is, will you go back for others? Time is short, lives are at stake—but do we see the urgency?

A MATTER OF LIFE AND DEATH

Jesus was on a rescue mission. He left the comfort of heaven to come to earth, to meet lost people so they could be saved. People like this unknown Samaritan. There was urgency about this work for Jesus. It was a matter of life and death.

This sense of urgency comes out in John 4:35:

> Don't you have a saying, 'It's still four months until harvest'? I tell you, open your eyes and look at the fields! They are ripe for harvest.

The harvest was ready now, not in four months' time. Crops that are ripe and are left in the field are in danger of being lost. Jesus wants the disciples to see that the time for action is *now*. They may never see that woman at the well, or the people of Sychar, again.

Evangelism is not something that can be put on hold; time is short. I wonder if we have lost this sense of urgency. Perhaps one of the reasons for this is that we have stopped really believing in the lostness of humanity. This is a doctrine that has been under attack from many different directions for many years. Liberalism has questioned a literal interpretation of the Bible's teaching on eternity. Universalism has questioned the existence of hell. Annihilationism has questioned the idea of a conscious eternal punishment.

But Jesus is very clear. He warns of being 'thrown into hell, where "the worms that eat them do not die, and the fire is not quenched"' (Mark 9:47b–48). In Luke 16 Jesus tells the story of the rich man and Lazarus. The rich man ends up in hell, which is clearly a conscious experience, and one that is final and eternal. It has been said that Jesus spoke more of hell than he did of heaven. The rest of the Bible is clear, too. In Revelation 20 we read,

The lake of fire is the second death. Anyone whose name was not found written in the book of life was thrown into the lake of fire (vv. 14–15).

C. T. Studd, the pioneer missionary, once wrote:

I can easily see why the folks at home want to eliminate hell from their theology, preaching and thought. Hell is indeed awful, unless its preaching is joined to a life laid down by the preacher. How can man believe in hell unless he throws away his life to rescue others from its torment? If there is no hell, the Bible is a lie. If we are not willing to go to hell on earth for others, we cannot preach it.

The story is told of Charlie Peace, a violent criminal who was sentenced to death in my own city of Leeds in the early twentieth century. He was placed in the condemned cell of Armley Jail (Leeds Prison) for twenty-nine days. This was meant to be a time for repentance, but Charlie Peace went to the cell bragging that he wasn't afraid to die. On the day of his execution, there was a procession from the cell to the gallows. A priest who was reading passages from the Bible led Charlie Peace. Suddenly, Peace stopped the proceedings. Grabbing the priest by the arm he said, 'Did you just read something from the Bible about hell being a lake of everlasting fire? Is that the hell of the Bible?'

'That is what it says,' replied the embarrassed priest.

'Well,' said Peace, 'if that is the true state of hell, then you could cover England in broken glass and say, "Charlie Peace, crawl on hands and knees from coast to coast [about 120 miles] and you will save your soul from hell," and I would say I would be a wise man to do it.'

In one sense, Charlie Peace was wrong. Nothing we can do will save a single soul from hell; only Jesus can do that. But, in another sense, he was right: no lengths are too great for us to go to, to show one person the way to eternal life.

The apostle Paul was one who was willing to be 'cursed' himself in order for others to escape hell. He wrote in his letter to the Romans:

> I speak the truth in Christ—I am not lying, my conscience confirms it through the Holy Spirit—I have great sorrow and unceasing anguish in my heart. For I could wish that I myself were cursed and cut off from Christ for the sake of my people, those of my own race, the people of Israel (Rom. 9:1–4).

Of course that could never happen to Paul, but he was sincere when he said it. Paul was demonstrating a Christlike sacrificial love. At the cross, Christ did literally go through hell so others could escape it.

In his letter, Jude tells Christians to 'save others by snatching them from the fire' (v. 23). That is what we are doing when we share the gospel and lead others to Christ.

ONLY ONE WAY

We also lose our sense of urgency to share the gospel when we stop believing in the uniqueness of Christ as the way of salvation. In Acts 4 Peter and John are arrested for preaching the gospel and are dragged before the Sanhedrin, the Jewish ruling council. The council threaten the apostles and command them to stop spreading the message of Jesus. Peter boldly declares the truth that Christ is the only way to be saved:

Salvation is found in no one else, for there is no other name under heaven given to mankind by which we must be saved (Acts 4:12).

This truth cuts right across our pluralistic and relativistic age. We are either being told that all religions are equally valid and no one has a monopoly on the truth; or that there is no such thing as an absolute truth. Either way, we are told, to preach Christ as the only way to God and heaven is invalid. Nevertheless, it may not be politically correct in the eyes of many today, but it is biblically correct, and that is what matters. If this message of Jesus really is the unique way to God, then we must tell it; that was in part what motivated those early preachers. This conviction—that it is only through calling on the name of Christ that we can be saved—is echoed in Paul's words in Romans 10:

For there is no difference between Jew and Gentile—the same Lord is Lord of all and richly blesses all who call on him, for, 'Everyone who calls on the name of the Lord will be saved.'

How, then, can they call on the one they have not believed in? And how can they believe in the one of whom they have not heard? And how can they hear without someone preaching to them? And how can anyone preach unless they are sent? As it is written: 'How beautiful are the feet of those who bring good news!' (Rom. 10:12–15).

The logic is simple. It is essential we tell others about Christ, for people cannot believe in someone they have not heard of, and they cannot be saved if they do not call on him. That Christ is the only way to salvation becomes one of the great motivations for urgency in our witness.

One Mercedes-Benz TV commercial shows their car

surviving a collision with a cement wall during a safety test. Someone then asks the company spokesman why Mercedes-Benz does not enforce its patent on the energy-absorbing car body, a design evidently copied by other companies because of its success. The spokesman replies matter-of-factly, 'Because some things in life are too important not to share.' The message that Christ alone can save falls, more than anything else, into the category of 'things too important not to share'.

If you or I were to discover the cure for cancer, we would want to get that lifesaving message to as many people as quickly as possible. To do anything else would be irresponsible and cruel. Yet we have in the gospel the only cure to the world's worst condition. Sin is universal; it affects everyone; and it is always fatal. Christ is the only remedy. To keep that cure to ourselves is irresponsible and cruel. May God help us all to see the urgency of getting this message to as many as possible, as quickly as possible.

Personal or group study: 2 Corinthians 5:11–20

1. *What motivates Paul in his evangelistic ministry (vv. 11a, 14)?*
2. *How does Paul describe his gospel appeal (v. 20)?*
3. *Why can the idea of being God's ambassador in the world encourage you to be bold?*
4. *How does the sacrifice of Jesus on the cross encourage us to tell others, whatever they might think of us (vv. 14–15)?*

9 Boldness: How to be a courageous witness

Within minutes of becoming a believer the Samaritan woman is witnessing. It doesn't matter how long you have been converted, you can be a witness—and a powerful one. This woman shows a remarkable boldness for someone who has known Christ for such a short time.

There are many reasons why we don't witness, but perhaps, if we are honest, one of the main reasons is fear. So what is the secret of this kind of boldness that overcomes our fear?

In Acts 4 there is a powerful example of courageous witnessing. Peter and John have just been arrested by the temple guard for preaching the gospel to a large crowd outside the temple gates. They are thrown into prison overnight and the next morning hauled before the Sanhedrin. Far from being intimidated by this gathering, Peter boldly preaches the gospel to the council, defending their right to carry on telling others the message. The impression that the apostles make on the Sanhedrin is profound:

> When they saw *the courage* of Peter and John and realized that they were unschooled, ordinary men, they were astonished and they took note that these men had been with Jesus (Acts 4:13, emphasis added).

It is the courage not just of the apostles that is highlighted in this chapter, but of all the other believers who gathered after Peter and John's release:

> And they were all filled with the Holy Spirit and *spoke the word of God boldly* (v. 31, emphasis added).

What lies behind this bold witnessing? Why were these messengers of the gospel so unstoppable?

Perhaps it is worth noting first of all what it was not. It was not that they were just naturally courageous. It is significant that Peter, the one at the very centre of the story, was the very one who just seven weeks earlier had totally failed to speak up for Jesus. On the night of Christ's arrest Peter had followed the guards taking Jesus to the high priest's house. While Christ was being interrogated inside, Peter was warming himself by a fire in the courtyard with some of the high priest's servants. Three times he was asked if he was one of Jesus' followers, and three times he denied it. Peter, frozen with fear, had been intimidated into silence. Clearly something other than just a naturally courageous disposition is being demonstrated now in Acts 4.

Neither can we attribute the bold witness of the disciples to exceptional intelligence or learning. In fact, it is the very absence of this in Peter and John that strikes the members of the Sanhedrin. It is their very ordinariness that makes what they did so extraordinary.

CONFIDENCE IN GOD

We can sum up the source of their courage in two ways. First, their confidence was in and from God. It was supernatural boldness. When Peter stood before the Sanhedrin to make his case, we read:

Then Peter, *filled with the Holy Spirit*, said to them: 'Rulers and elders of the people!' (v. 8, emphasis added).

Peter's power did not come from himself; he was empowered by the Holy Spirit. The same thing is said of the rest of the believers:

And they were all *filled with the Holy Spirit* and spoke the word of God boldly (v. 31, emphasis added).

Throughout the book of Acts, the Spirit and witnessing are linked. It is one of the key themes of the whole book. It is introduced at the start with Christ's instructions to his disciples:

But you will receive power when the Holy Spirit comes on you; and you will be my witnesses in Jerusalem, and in all Judea and Samaria, and to the ends of the earth (Acts 1:8).

When the Spirit comes, the witnesses go. This is the acid test for every movement that claims to be Spirit-filled and Spirit-led: is it characterized by bold witnessing? Our witnessing will never be bold unless it is done in conscious dependence on God's power.

This sense of God-dependence also comes out in the way those early disciples prayed.

'Sovereign Lord,' they said, 'you made the heaven and the earth and the sea, and everything in them. You spoke by the Holy Spirit through the mouth of your servant, our father David:

> "Why do the nations rage
>   and the peoples plot in vain?
> The kings of the earth rise up
>   and the rulers band together
> against the Lord
>   and against his anointed one."
>
> Indeed Herod and Pontius Pilate met together with the Gentiles and the people of Israel in this city to conspire against your holy servant Jesus, whom you anointed. They did what your power and will had decided beforehand should happen. Now, Lord, consider their threats and enable your servants to speak your word with great boldness' (Acts 4:24–29).

They had a big view of God in their praying. He was the 'Sovereign Lord'. That view of God helped them to see their opponents from the right perspective. With this God on their side they had no logical reason to fear. This was God's world, he had made it, and so they had every right to speak his word to everyone. I find it helpful to remember this when I feel I am invading people's personal territory when I speak to them of Christ. We have every right to do so because it is not their personal territory: it is God's. The very air they breathe comes from God; their lives belong to him by right. It is also important to remember, as these early believers did, that God is in ultimate control of every circumstance and situation. They didn't need to feel intimidated by the Sanhedrin or any other authority, because God sovereignly ruled over them all. Even their attempts to undermine God's saving plan would work for it in the end. That means that ultimately we cannot fail in gospel work.

When I was involved in a university mission a number of

years ago I was asked to give an impromptu short talk in the student refectory. It was a riot. Within seconds of my getting up on one of the tables to speak, food began to fly through the air in my direction. After just a few minutes I beat a hasty retreat. The whole thing seemed to be a very embarrassing waste of time. However, one young man who witnessed the whole thing decided he would attend that evening's mission event, on the basis that if I was willing to stand up and take that abuse, I must have something worth saying. That night he trusted Christ. God can use our very opponents to bring about his work.

It is these convictions about God that can give us the courage to speak his word boldly, just as those first believers did. As we step out in dependence on him we can expect his Spirit to enable and empower us.

CONFIDENCE IN THE GOSPEL MESSAGE

The second reason for the boldness of Peter and John was their confidence in the gospel. They had a deep and unshakeable conviction that the message of Jesus was both true and of supreme importance.

> ... know this, you and all the people of Israel: it is by the name of Jesus Christ of Nazareth, whom you crucified but whom God raised from the dead, that this man stands before you healed. Jesus is
>
> 'the stone you builders rejected,
> which has become the cornerstone.'
>
> Salvation is found in no one else, for there is no other name under heaven given to mankind by which we must be saved (Acts 4:10–12).

They confidently speak of Jesus as both a real man and really God. He is both Jesus of Nazareth and the Christ, God's Anointed. They speak of the facts of both his crucifixion and his resurrection. They speak of the choice all have to reject him and be lost or to trust him and be saved. That is the choice, for there is no other way. This is a great statement of gospel truth. When they are told to stop speaking this message, they reply,

> Which is right in God's eyes: to listen to you, or to him? You be the judges! As for us, we cannot help speaking about what we have seen and heard (vv. 19–20).

They cannot stop telling the message, for they cannot deny its truth or its importance. It is only when we share these deep convictions about the gospel that we are going to keep on evangelizing. It is a confidence in the gospel that will give us confidence to witness.

There is another reason for confidence in the gospel: it is a powerful message. At the beginning of Acts 4 we read that Peter and John are seized and put in jail. The very next verse says, 'But many who heard the message believed; so the number of men who believed grew to about five thousand' (v. 4). It's as if Luke is saying: you can lock up the messengers, but you can't lock up the message. Paul, writing from prison to encourage young Timothy, says something very similar:

> Remember Jesus Christ, raised from the dead, descended from David. This is my gospel, for which I am suffering even to the point of being chained like a criminal. But God's word is not chained (2 Tim. 2:8–9).

Paul is reminding Timothy that, although the authorities can imprison the messenger, they cannot lock up the message. The gospel message is unstoppable. At the beginning of his great epistle about the gospel, Paul says the reason why he is not ashamed to preach the gospel is because it is 'the power of God that brings salvation to everyone who believes' (Rom. 1:16). The message is powerful.

This is a repeated theme in the book of Acts. The phrase 'the word of God spread' comes a number of times. It's interesting to notice the context of these occurrences.

> So the word of God spread. The number of disciples in Jerusalem increased rapidly, and a large number of priests became obedient to the faith (Acts 6:7).

You might expect priests to be hard nuts to crack, but here we read that a large number are converted as they hear the powerful gospel message.

> On the appointed day Herod, wearing his royal robes, sat on his throne and delivered a public address to the people. They shouted, 'This is the voice of a god, not of a man.' Immediately, because Herod did not give praise to God, an angel of the Lord struck him down, and he was eaten by worms and died.
>
> But the word of God continued to spread and flourish (12:21–24).

There is a powerful contrast in these verses. Herod, a vicious opponent of the gospel, is stuck down and silenced, but the message he so proudly opposed goes on doing its powerful work. Long after today's opponents of the gospel have gone, the gospel will continue to change lives.

> Many of those who believed now came and openly confessed what they had done. A number who had practised sorcery

> brought their scrolls together and burned them publicly. When they calculated the value of the scrolls, the total came to fifty thousand drachmas. In this way the word of the Lord spread widely and grew in power (19:18–20).

This time the context is the conversion of the Ephesians who had been involved in pagan occult practices. They publicly burn the valuable sorcery scrolls to show everyone the change Christ has made. Again we see the life-transforming power of the gospel in the very heart of a satanic stronghold.

When we tell the gospel, we are sharing a powerful message. God will do a powerful work through it. C. H. Spurgeon, the famous nineteenth-century preacher, was once listening to some younger men bemoaning the lack of converts in their ministry.

'You don't expect people to be saved every time you preach, do you?' said Spurgeon.

'Oh no,' they insisted.

'Well, that's your problem!' he replied.

We will have a greater boldness in our witnessing if, like Peter and John and those other early believers in Acts 4, our confidence is in a powerful God and his powerful gospel.

Personal or group study: Romans 1:1–17

1. *Why is Paul not ashamed of the gospel (v. 16)?*
2. *How does Paul describe his attitude to going to Rome, and why does he feel that way (vv. 14–15)?*
3. *What is it about the gospel that should give us great confidence to share it (vv. 1–6, 17)?*

10 Rewards: It's worth it!

Even now the one who reaps draws a wage and harvests a crop for eternal life, so that the sower and the reaper may be glad together (John 4:36).

Soul-winning work is costly, but it is also immensely rewarding. The image Jesus uses in John 4 of the harvest is a good illustration of this. When I was a boy, at harvest time, I would go and help on a farm near to where I lived. We spent long hours in the fields stacking straw bales. They were heavy and prickled the skin on your arms mercilessly; however, at the end of a long day it was very satisfying to look back at the fields of neatly stacked bales—and also to get the few pounds we were paid for the work. Harvesting can be back-breaking work, but it is worth it.

ETERNAL REWARDS

Jesus speaks of the rewards of being involved in harvesting souls. There are rewards in this work that you will not find in any other activity of life. These rewards, says Jesus, are eternal. Nothing in life will have longer-lasting effects than reaching others for Christ.

It will not be until we reach heaven that the true rewards of gospel ministry will be experienced. Firstly, and most importantly, there will be the 'Well done!' from the Master for obedient service. This should matter to us more than anything else.

The story is told of an elderly couple returning from Africa after many years of missionary service on that continent. It was before the days of plane travel so they were travelling by passenger liner back to the USA. It just so happened that the President of the USA was also travelling on board. When the ship docked in New York harbour there was a great commotion on the dockside as the President disembarked. A band played as the press snapped their photos. Finally, it was the turn of the rest of the passengers to leave. By this point, the band had gone, as had the photographers. Unlike for the President, there was no grand home-coming reception for the missionary couple: they slipped away unnoticed with the rest of the passengers. That night, the elderly missionary confided to his wife his disappointment at the reception they had received on their return, in such stark contrast to that received by the President returning from his holidays. He knew it was wrong but he couldn't shake off the bitterness. 'Go and pray about it,' she replied. A while later he returned to the room, beaming. When his wife asked how he had got on, he replied, 'The Lord told me that we're not home yet!'

Faithful gospel ministry is not appreciated much these days; in fact, you are more likely to be criticized by the world than celebrated. But remember: you're not home yet. A day is coming when all our service for God will be recognized. Sometimes we struggle with the idea of rewards in heaven, but we shouldn't: it is something Jesus taught. The thought that Christ will one day commend those who have served him should motivate us.

There will also be the reward of seeing those in whose coming to faith we were privileged to play some part. It has been said that the only thing you can take to heaven with you is someone else. Paul speaks of this reward when he writes to the Thessalonians:

> For what is our hope, our joy, or the crown in which we will glory in the presence of our Lord Jesus when he comes? Is it not you? (1 Thes. 2:19).

Sir Nicholas George Winton MBE is a British humanitarian who organized the rescue of 669 mostly Jewish children from Nazi-occupied Czechoslovakia on the eve of the Second World War, in an operation later known as the 'Czech Kindertransport'. 'Winton found homes for the children and arranged for their safe passage to Britain … The British press dubbed him the "British Schindler".'[1]

Winton kept quiet about his humanitarian exploits for many years, until 1988, when his wife, Grete,

> found a detailed scrapbook in their attic, containing lists of the children, including their parents' names and the names and addresses of the families that took them in … Letters were sent to each of these known addresses and 80 of 'Winton's children' were found in Britain. The wider world found out about his work in February 1988 during an episode of the BBC television programme *That's Life!* when he was invited as a member of the audience. At one point, Winton's scrapbook was shown and his achievements were explained. The host of the programme, Esther Rantzen, asked whether anybody in the audience owed their lives to Winton, and if so, to stand—more than two dozen people surrounding Winton rose and applauded.[2]

Winston stood and gazed around at the smiling faces of those he had played a part in saving, joy and surprise on his face, and tears in his eyes. That was a very moving TV moment;

but imagine the scene in eternity when you and I meet people that we played a part, under God, in bringing to faith!

THE JOY OF THE HARVEST

However, I am sure part of the reward is experienced now. There is a wonderful satisfaction in knowing that you are involved in something that is truly of lasting value. Whether we are the sower or the reaper, Jesus says we can be glad together. In each of the three parables in Luke 15—the lost sheep, coin and son—there is great rejoicing when that which was lost is found. There is joy in winning others for Christ that few other things in life can match. Although gospel ministry can at times be very costly, it is also hugely fulfilling.

Towards the end of her life Gladys Aylward, who had been a missionary to China for many years, gave an address back home in Britain. In part of this talk she spoke of the hardships she had faced during her long years on the mission field:

> I have not done what I wanted to. I have not eaten what I wanted or worn what I would have chosen. I have lived in houses that I would not have looked at twice. I longed for a husband and babies and security and love. But God never gave them. Instead, he left me alone for seventeen years with one book, a Chinese Bible. I don't know anything about the latest novels, pictures, and theatres. I live in a rather out-of-date world. And I suppose you say it's awful miserable, isn't it? Friend, I have been one of the happiest women that have ever stepped this earth. I've known the heavens opening and the blessing tumbling out.[3]

The apostle Paul speaks of the joy of making sacrifices for the spiritual blessing of others when he writes to the Philippians:

> But even if I am being poured out like a drink offering on the sacrifice and service coming from your faith, I am glad and rejoice with all of you (Phil. 2:17).

Paul was in prison for preaching the gospel when he penned those words. He faced possible execution, yet he was able to speak of his joy at knowing that all his suffering had been for the eternal blessing of others. Paul knew there really was no greater cause to give your life for than that.

In the early 1980s, Steve Jobs wanted John Sculley, the then President of Pepsi, to join Apple and 'apply his marketing skills to the personal computer market. Steve Jobs successfully sealed the deal after he made his legendary pitch to John: "Do you want to sell sugared water for the rest of your life? Or do you want to come with me and change the world?"'[4] Likewise, Jesus calls us to leave our small ambitions and give our lives to changing the world by reaching lost people. But as we give ourselves to this ministry, we will be changing the very eternal destinies of men and women. There is no greater work to which any of us can give ourselves. Are you willing to get involved? It's going to be costly—at times frustrating and even heart-breaking; but it will be worth it.

In Chapter 2 I mentioned my furniture-restoring friend who works for the Queen. I am sure he would say that it is a great feeling to see a piece on which he has spent hours working, restored and put back in those staterooms in Windsor Castle where it belongs. One day, we will be where we belong for all eternity—heaven—and it's going to be breathtaking. We will look at one another and be amazed at the transformation. But remember where all that furniture-rescue work began:

among the dust and shavings of the workshop, restoring and reclaiming what was damaged and broken. That is where you and I are right now. This is the workshop, and all around us are broken people who need rescuing.

So what are you waiting for? Roll up your sleeves and get involved!

Revive us, Lord! Is zeal abating
While harvest fields are vast and white?
Revive us, Lord, the world is waiting;
Equip thy church to spread the light.[5]

Notes

1 'Nicholas Winton', Wikipedia (last modified 28 Aug. 2016), https://en.wikipedia.org/wiki/Nicholas_Winton.

2 Ibid.

3 Words from a tape recording I have of a talk she once gave (no date).

4 'John Sculley', Wikipedia (last modified 31 Aug. 2016), https://en.wikipedia.org/wiki/John_Sculley.

5 Bessie P. Head, 'O Breath of Life', c.1914.

Appendix: Answers to study questions

Chapter 1: Jonah 4

1. Nineveh was the capital of the Assyrian Empire, an avowed enemy of Israel. The prophet Jonah was a fiercely patriotic Israelite. Jonah ran from God's call, not because he was afraid of a negative reaction to God's warning of judgement on Nineveh, but because he feared a positive one. The last thing Jonah wanted was for the Ninevites to heed God's warning and repent. Jonah knew that God is compassionate and merciful, and would forgive the Ninevites if they did repent. That is exactly what happened, and what he bitterly bemoans in chapter 4. Jonah disobeyed God in chapter 1, not out of cowardice, but out of callousness.
2. The mercy and compassion of God should cause us too to be merciful and compassionate. Just as God's compassion extends to all people, no matter how bad, so should ours.
3. God used the loss of the leafy plant that gave shade to Jonah from the sun to show how selfish his attitude to the Ninevites had been. Jonah cared more that he escaped the heat of the sun for a day, than he did that a whole city should escape God's judgement for ever.
4. If we prioritize our personal popularity or comfort over the spiritual needs of others we will stop evangelizing once it becomes difficult or unpopular.

Chapter 2: 1 Corinthians 9:19–23; 10:31–33

1. Paul describes himself as a slave to unsaved people. A slave lives for the welfare of his master. Paul is saying that he lives for the spiritual welfare of non-Christians. His reason for doing this is that they may be converted and saved.
2. Putting the welfare of non-Christians before his own means that Paul is

willing constantly to adapt and change to each new situation in order that he may more effectively relate to non-Christians from different backgrounds. Paul is willing to put aside his own personal preferences and practices for the sake of reaching others with the gospel.

3. This principled pragmatic approach may mean we are willing to go to places and do things that wouldn't necessarily be our personal preference, in order to get alongside non-Christians. It means we will spend time finding out what others enjoy, or don't enjoy, and adapt our lifestyles in order to befriend others.
4. These verses act as a check on going too far in this pragmatic approach, by reminding us that everything we do must still be done to the glory of God. If adapting to others leads to compromising with sin, it obviously cannot be done to the glory of God. We are also reminded here that we must not cause anyone to stumble spiritually, including other Christians.

Chapter 3: Acts 8:26–40

1. God is able to lead Philip to the right person at the right time with the right words. Although we cannot expect to be supernaturally transported as he was, we can pray that God would lead us to people and situations where we will have opportunities to speak for him. We can also pray that God will give us wisdom in answering their questions.
2. God was already at work in the Ethiopian's heart long before Philip met him on the road. He is already reading God's Word and asking searching questions before Philip has the opportunity to say anything. God is always working in different people's lives to cause them to seek him, long before we know it or even know them. Our part is to be ready to tell them the answers in the gospel when we have opportunity.
3. Philip hears the Ethiopian reading from Isaiah 53 and so he begins with the questions the Ethiopian is asking about that passage. Although there is one gospel message for everyone, each person has a different level of interest and understanding. Before we start speaking we need to ask questions and listen to find out where people are, so we can be relevant

and helpful to them as individuals. We need to start where they are, not where we think they ought to be.

4. Philip wasn't expecting that conversation at the start of the day; it was a God-arranged appointment. But when the opportunity arose he was ready to take it. None of us know who we might meet and what conversations we might have on any given day; the important thing is to be ready every day to share something of the gospel as the God-given opportunities arise.

Chapter 5: Romans 3:21–26

1. The gospel is a universal message that all need to hear because it answers a universal problem we all have: sin and its judgement.
2. The universal solution to that problem is what Jesus did on the cross: his taking the punishment for that sin, so we can be made right with God (justified) and rescued from sin's guilt and power (redeemed). All this comes to us as we simply put our trust (faith) in what he has done for us (grace), not in what we can do for him.
3. Failing to tell people about their sin is like offering the cure to a disease to people who are totally unaware they are sick. How will people see the need for a Saviour if they are unaware they need saving? They would be entitled to say, 'That's fine for you, but it's not for me; I'm happy as I am'—which is exactly what a lot of people do say. Once people are aware of their sin, however, the offer of forgiveness becomes very relevant.
4. Jesus had to die for our forgiveness because God's justice demands that sin be punished. God couldn't overlook our sin for ever, so Jesus took that punishment at the cross in our place so that we don't need to. So God shows he is righteous by punishing sin and that he is right when he doesn't punish those who have put their trust in Jesus.
5. The response God wants to the gospel message is faith. Faith is simply putting your trust in Jesus to do for you what you cannot do for yourself.

Chapter 7: Acts 26:1–29

1. Paul describes himself as a religious fanatic who persecuted Christians. He

openly and honestly admits to being responsible for the imprisonment and death of believers.

2. Paul describes what happened in some detail. He explains what he heard, saw and thought. He explains how his understanding of who Jesus is changed and what that was going to mean for him for the rest of his life. He put Jesus in the spotlight, not himself. He shows that becoming a Christian was more than something intellectual, the conviction of some truths; it was a personal and life-changing encounter with the living Lord.
3. Paul shows that repentance (turning from sin) and being obedient to Jesus as Lord are both essential to living the Christian life. In other words, becoming a Christian isn't just a ticket to heaven when we die; it's a new way of living before we die.
4. Paul ends his testimony with a challenge to those listening that this is something they need themselves.

Chapter 8: 2 Corinthians 5:11–20

1. Paul's evangelistic ministry is motivated by both a reverence for God—'fear the Lord', which leads to a desire to please God—and the love of God.
2. Paul's gospel appeal is passionate, urgent and persuasive: 'We implore you.' He doesn't leave people in any doubt as to what they must do and that doing it is vitally important.
3. The concept of being God's ambassador should encourage us to be bold because it implies we have an authority that comes from the one we represent, God. We are not representing our own ideas on our own initiative; we are delivering God's message at his initiative. This has got to be one of the greatest privileges anyone could be given.
4. The sacrifice of Jesus on the cross should encourage us to tell others. Because he was willing to die for us, we should be willing to give ourselves for him and others.

Chapter 9: Romans 1:1–17

1. Paul is not ashamed of the gospel because it is God's message that has the power to save everyone who believes.

2. Paul is eager to go to Rome because it will mean he can fulfil his responsibility to preach the good news to everyone there. Rome did not faze Paul, even though it was the centre of power for the Roman Empire, because he knew he represented a higher power.
3. The gospel message itself should give us confidence to proclaim it because it is God's message—'the gospel of God' (v. 1)—from God's Word—'the Holy Scriptures' (v. 2)—about God's Son (v. 3) and proved to be true by the resurrection (v. 4). The gospel message is the only way we can get right with God (v. 17).